STUDENT'S BOOK

English Explorer 1

Helen Stephenson

NATIONAL GEOGRAPHIC LEARNING | CENGAGE Learning

Australia • Brazil • Japan • Korea • Mexico • Singapore • Spain • United Kingdom • United States

Contents

Skills: Listening & Speaking	Pronunciation	Culture & CLIL
Listening: Classroom instructions **Speaking:** Saying your name		
Listening: A description of a family People at a library **Speaking:** Making introductions Giving personal information	Intonation in questions	Greenwich: where time begins CLIL: Geography and English Time zones
Listening: Teenagers talking about their parents **Speaking:** Making requests Giving dates	*can* and *can't*	Amazing animals CLIL: Biology and English Animal facts
Listening: Personal information **Speaking:** Talking about favourite activities Ordering a meal	*th* and *t*	Food in the UK CLIL: Biology and English A balanced diet
Listening: An interview **Speaking:** Talking about daily routines	Words with /ɜː/	Olympic athletes CLIL: Maths and English Statistics
Listening: A radio programme **Speaking:** Making suggestions Describing pictures	Intonation in questions The /ə/ sound	Houses and homes CLIL: Geography and English Climate change
Listening: A clothing analyst explaining what our clothes say about us **Speaking:** Talking about plans Buying things	Sentence stress The unstressed /ɪ/ sound	UNICEF and schools CLIL: Social Science and English NGOs
Listening: A biography **Speaking:** Talking about past activities Making, accepting or declining invitations	*-ed* endings	Festivals with fire CLIL: Chemistry and English Fire
Listening: Information from a museum **Speaking:** Asking about events in the past Telling stories	The /ɔː/ sound	Astronomers CLIL: Science and English The solar system

Starter My classroom

1 S1 **Listen and repeat**

1	a board	9	a ruler
2	a door	10	a notebook
3	a wall	11	a desk
4	a window	12	a bag
5	a teacher	13	a chair
6	a student	14	a pen
7	a pencil	15	a rubber
8	a book	16	a dictionary

2 S2 **Cover the word box in Exercise 1. Look at the picture. Listen and say the number.**

3 Work in pairs.

A: Say a number.

B: Cover the word box. Say the word.

e.g. A: 12

B: a bag

Take turns.

4 Write six things you can see in your classroom.

e.g. a window, ...

The alphabet

5 S3 **Listen and repeat.**

A B C D E F G H I J K L M N

a b c d e f g h i j k l m n

O P Q R S T U V W X Y Z

o p q r s t u v w x y z

6 S4 **Listen and write the words.**

e.g. desk

7 **Look at the picture on page 4. Work in pairs and test your partner.**

e.g. A: How do you spell 'board'?
B: B-O-A-R-D.
A: Yes!

8 **Spell your name.**

Numbers

9 S5 **Listen and repeat.**

1	one	11	eleven
2	two	12	twelve
3	three	13	thirteen
4	four	14	fourteen
5	five	15	fifteen
6	six	16	sixteen
7	seven	17	seventeen
8	eight	18	eighteen
9	nine	19	nineteen
10	ten	20	twenty

10 **Match the numbers with the words.**

a	30	**1**	ninety
b	40	**2**	fifty
c	50	**3**	one hundred
d	60	**4**	forty
e	70	**5**	sixty
f	80	**6**	eighty
g	90	**7**	seventy
h	100	**8**	thirty

11 **Do the maths and write the numbers.**

a 11 x 5 =
b 7 x 9 =
c 15 x 4 =
d 45 x 2 =

12 **Write the number of …**

1. pages in this unit. ....
2. students in your classroom. ....
3. windows in your classroom. ....
4. teachers in your school. ....

Plurals

13 S6 **Study the table and write these words in the correct box. Then listen, check and repeat.**

Add *-s* to most singular nouns	toy – toys
After *-s*, *-sh*, *-ch*, *-x* and *-o* endings, add *–es*	box – boxes
After a consonant + *-y* ending, change -y to *–ies*	family – families

baby **computer** **glass** **key** **library** **phone** **party** **potato** **umbrella** **watch**

Colours

14 **Write the colours.**

1. blue + yellow =
2. red + yellow =
3. blue + red =

15 **Write the number of …**

1. blue books in your classroom.
2. brown desks in your classroom.
3. black watches in your classroom.
4. red pencils in your classroom.

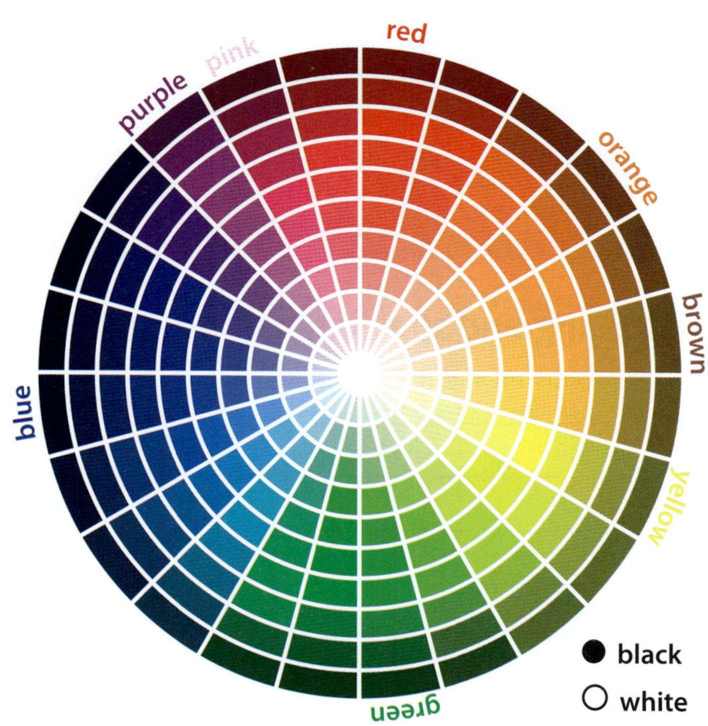

Starter My school

Listening and speaking

1 S7 **Listen and tick the names.**

Daniel	
Jane	
Katherine	
Mr Wilson	✓
Peter	
Robert	
Charlotte	

2 S8 **Listen and repeat.**

Charlotte: I'm Charlotte. What's your name?
Robert: My name's Robert.
Charlotte: Hi, Robert.
Robert: Hello, Charlotte.

3 **What's your name? Work in pairs and tell your partner.**

e.g. A: Hello, I'm ...
B: Hi, my name's ...

Subject pronouns

4 **Find the subject pronouns and complete the sentences.**

1 ....'s a book.
2 ....'re teachers.
3 ....'re pens.
4 ....'m Charlotte.

Time

5 S9 **Listen and repeat.**

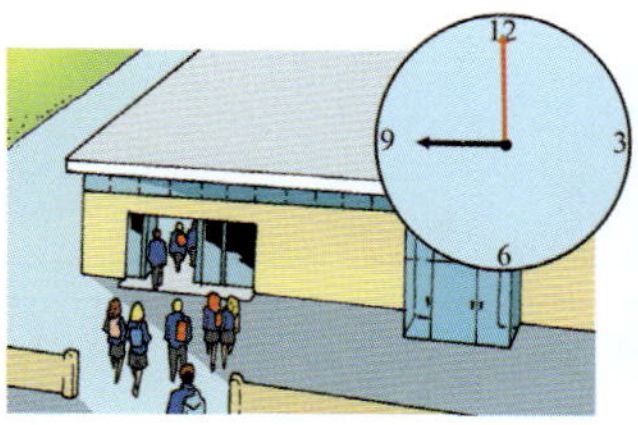
It's nine o'clock.

It's half past ten.

It's quarter past twelve.

It's quarter to four.

6 S10 **Listen and number the clocks. Say the times.**

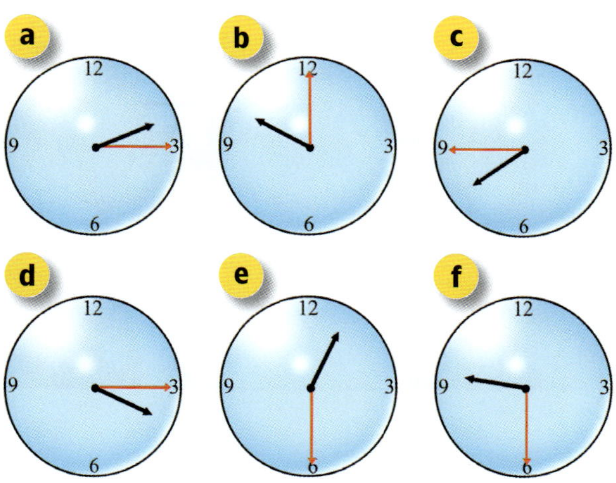

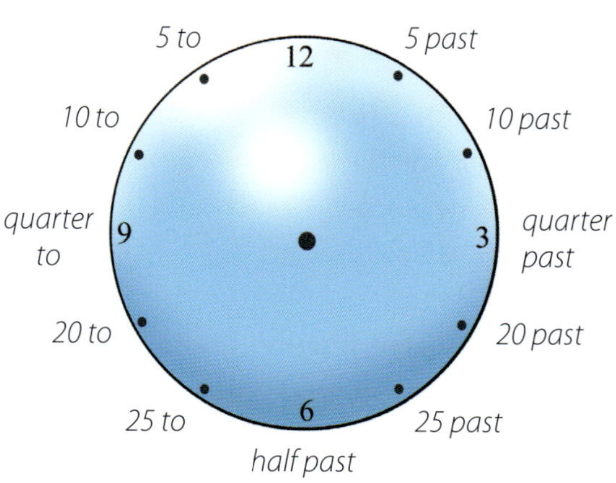

7 **Work in pairs.**

A: Draw six clocks with times. Say the times.
B: Listen and draw the clocks.

Compare your clocks. Take turns.

Days and months

September

M		6	13	20	27
T		7	14	21	28
W	1	8	15	22	29
T	2	9	16	23	30
F	3	10	17	24	
S	4	11	18	25	
S	5	12	19	26	

8 S11 **Write the days in the correct order. Then listen, check and repeat.**

Friday
Monday
Saturday
Sunday
Thursday
Tuesday
Wednesday

9 **Which days are school days?**

10 S12 **Write the months in the correct order. Listen, check and repeat.**

April
August
December
February
January
July
June
March
May
November
October
September

11 **Write the months.**

The school holidays
The new year
My birthday

12 **Write six months on a Bingo card. Then listen to your teacher.**

February		
	July	
		November

Starter Classroom language

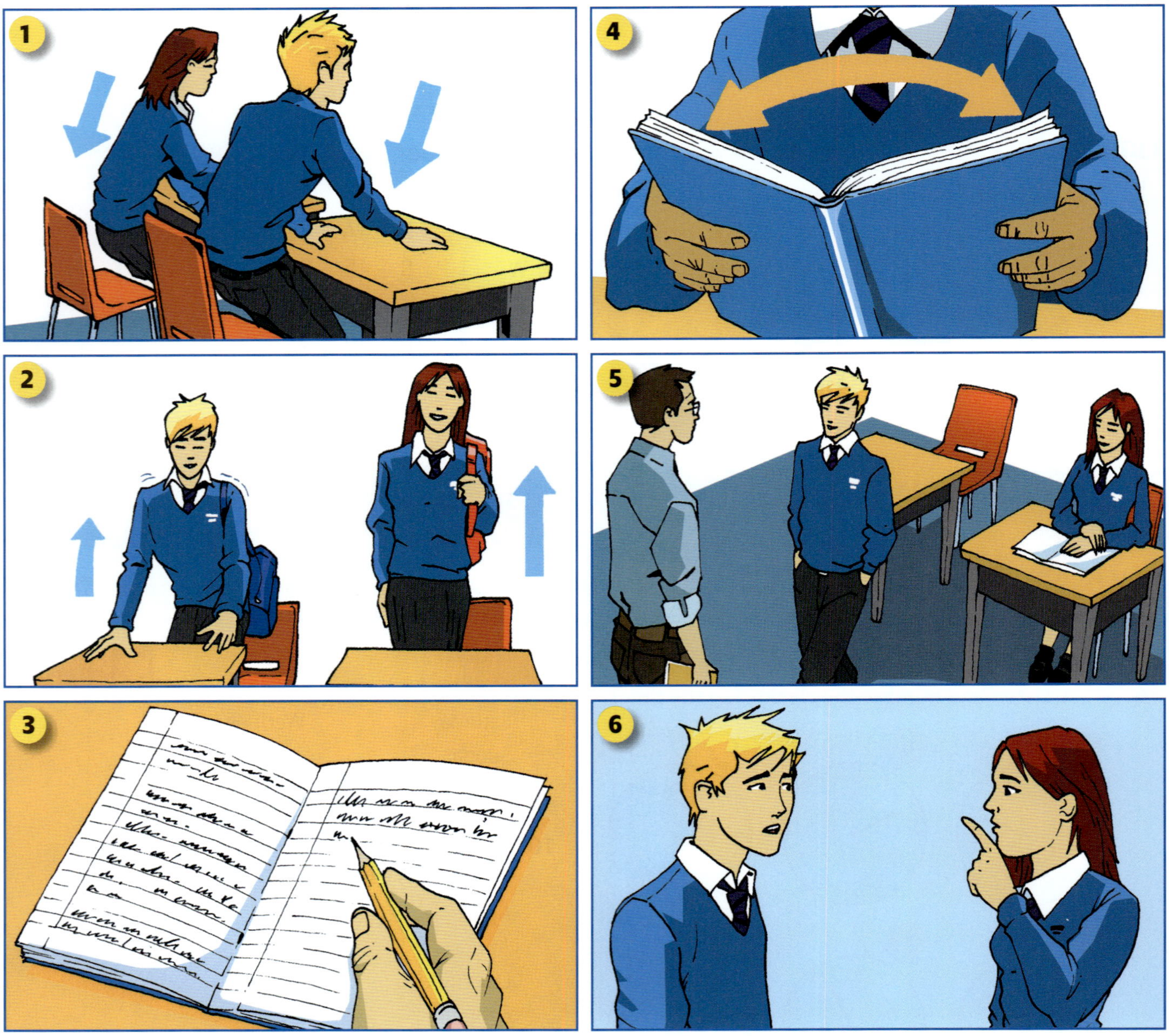

The imperative

1 S13 **Match the instructions with the pictures. Then listen and check.**

Stand up.	
Come here.	
Sit down.	1
Open your books.	
Don't talk.	
Write in your notebooks.	

2 S14 **Complete the instructions. Then listen and check.**

listen   open   ~~speak~~   study   watch   don't write

1 Speak English in class.
2 .... your notebooks.
3 .... to the teacher.
4 .... in the books.
5 .... at home.
6 .... films in English.

Affirmative
Open the book.
Negative
Don't open the book.

Classroom language: teacher

3 Write the sentences in your language.

Classroom language: student

4 Write the sentences in your language.

Starter Classroom language

1 S15 **Write T (teacher) or S (student). Then listen and check.**

1 Can I borrow a pen? S
2 Can you help me? ....
3 Do you understand? ....
4 I don't understand. ....
5 Finished. ....
6 Listen to me. ....
7 Look at the board. ....
8 Read in silence. ....
9 Work in pairs. ....
10 What does … mean, please? ....

2 Choose the correct words.

1 Greenwich is in New York / London.

6 Complete the sentences with short forms.

e.g. I 'm from Los Angeles.

1 He .... from the USA.

1 1.2 **Read and listen to the dialogue. Find the people in the photos.**

2 Read the text again and find their favourite things, a-c.

7 Study the table.

Negative		
I'm not You / We / They aren't He / She / It isn't	am not are not is not	English.

11 Put the words in order to make questions.

e.g. Brad / English / is? Is Brad English?

4 2.5 **Look at the pictures and write requests. Then listen, check and repeat.**

Exercise instructions

2 Write the sentences in your language.

1 Are the sentences true or false?
2 Ask and answer questions.
3 Choose the correct words.
4 Compare with your partner.
5 Complete the sentences.
6 Find the people in the photo.
7 Listen and check.
8 Listen and repeat.
9 Listen. Write the words you hear.
10 Look at the pictures.
11 Match the questions with the answers.
12 Put the words in order to make questions.
13 Read and listen to the dialogue.
14 Read the dialogue again. Complete the table.
15 Read the text.
16 Study the table.
17 Take turns.
18 Use your dictionary.
19 Work in pairs.
20 Write sentences with these words.

NATIONAL GEOGRAPHIC

My family and friends 1

> Grammar

Learn about *be*, possessive adjectives, and *this, that, these, those.*

> Vocabulary

Learn words for family relationships, describing appearance, and countries.

> Skills

Read about families, and about Greenwich and time zones.

Listen to a description of a family, and to people at a library.

Write personal information on a form.

> Communicate

Make introductions, and give personal information.

1 Describe what you can see in the picture.

2 1.1 Listen. Are they friends or family?

See Vocabulary Explorer: Page 98

3 Write the names of three English-speaking countries. For each country, write the capital, an animal, a famous person.

See Vocabulary Explorer: Page 99

1A Welcome!

Reading and listening

1 1.2 **Read and listen to the dialogue. Find the people in the photos.**

1

Meera: Is that Brad?
Anna: No, Brad's red-haired.
Harry: Is that Brad?
Anna: No, Brad's fourteen. That boy's ten or eleven!
Meera: Well, is that Brad?
Anna: No, Brad's tall and thin. He's a basketball player! He's American!

2

Anna: Hello, Brad! Welcome to London!
Brad: Hi, Anna. Thanks.
Anna: Brad, this is my friend Meera and her brother Harry.
Brad: Good afternoon!
Anna: Meera and Harry, this is my cousin Brad.
Harry: Hi! Nice to meet you!
Anna: Come on, Brad. Mum's over there.

3

Harry: Where are you from in the USA, Brad?
Brad: I'm from Los Angeles. And you?
Meera: We're from London.
Mum: Hello, Brad. Are you OK? Are you tired? Are you hungry?
Brad: Hi, Aunt Jane. Yes, I'm very hungry!

2 **Match the sentence beginnings (1–4) with the endings (a–d).**

1	Brad is b	a	cousins.
2	Anna and Meera are	b	a basketball player.
3	Meera and Harry are	c	friends.
4	Anna and Brad are	d	from London.

3 1.3 **Listen and repeat the introductions in Part 2 of the dialogue. Then work in groups of four and practise the introductions.**

Vocabulary

4 **Look at the people in the photo again. Choose the correct words.**

e.g. Harry is **short** / **tall.**

1. Brad is **red-haired / dark-haired.**
2. Brad is **short / tall.**
3. Brad is **fat / thin.**
4. Anna and her mother are **happy / sad.**
5. The suitcase is **big / small.**

See Vocabulary Explorer: Page 98

Grammar: *be* (affirmative)

5 **Read the dialogue again. Complete the table with short forms.**

Affirmative		
(1) .... You're (2) .... She's (3) .... (4) .... You're They're	I am You are He is She is It is We are You are They are	American.

See Grammar Explorer: Page 122

6 **Complete the sentences with short forms.**

e.g. I ...'m... from Los Angeles.

1. He .... from the USA.
2. They .... English.
3. We .... hungry.
4. I .... thirteen.
5. She .... fair.
6. You .... happy.

Grammar: *be* (negative)

7 **Study the table.**

Negative		
I'm not You/We/They aren't He/She/It isn't	am not are not is not	English.

See Grammar Explorer: Page 122

8 **Write the sentences in Exercise 6 with negative short forms.**

e.g. I'm not from Los Angeles.

9 **Write *is, isn't, are* or *aren't.***

Anna (**1**) .....is..... from Greenwich, in London. Her best friend (**2**) .... Meera. Anna and Brad (**3**) .... cousins. Brad (**4**) .... from London. He (**5**) .... from Los Angeles. Meera and Harry (**6**) .... cousins. They (**7**) .... brother and sister. They (**8**) .... English. They (**9**) .... American.

Grammar: *be* (questions and short answers)

10 **Study the table.**

Questions		
Am Are Is	I you/we/they he/she/it	Australian?

Short answers	
Yes, I am. Yes, you/we/they are. Yes, he/she/it is.	No, I'm not. No, you/we/they aren't. No, he/she/it isn't.

See Grammar Explorer: Page 122

11 **Put the words in order to make questions.**

e.g. Brad / English / is? Is Brad English?

1. friends / Meera and Anna / are?
2. twelve / is / Brad?
3. Harry and Meera / are / American?
4. Anna / from / London / is?
5. hungry / you / are?
6. we / students / are?

Fast finishers

Work in pairs. Ask and answer the questions in Exercise 11.

A: Is Brad English?
B: No, he isn't.

1B This is my family

Reading and listening

1 1.4 **Read and listen to the dialogue. Find the people in the photos.**

Brad: Well, I'm from Los Angeles, and this is my family.

Harry: Are they from Los Angeles too?

Brad: Yes, we're all from Los Angeles, except my mum. She's from London. That's my mum and that's my dad. Their names are Martha and Clark. They're scientists. At the moment, they're in Antarctica!

Harry: Who's that?

Brad: That's my aunt. Her name is Lena. She and my dad are sister and brother. That's my grandmother. Her name is Eve. She's seventy-five! And that's her cat.

Harry: What's its name?

Brad: Fluffy.

2 Complete the sentences about Brad and his family.

1 Brad is from ....
2 His mum is from ....
3 His mum and dad are ....
4 Lena is his ....
5 Eve is his ....
6 Fluffy is a ....

Listening

3 1.5 **Listen to Harry. Where is his family from? Choose the correct answer.**

a India
b Australia
c the USA

4 1.5 **Listen again. Are the sentences true or false?**

1	Harry and Meera are from London.	T / F
2	Their father is a teacher.	T / F
3	Their mother is a doctor.	T / F
4	Their grandparents are Indian.	T / F
5	Their grandmothers are sixty-nine.	T / F
6	Their uncle Deepak is in New Delhi.	T / F

Vocabulary

5 **Find the family words in Exercises 1 and 4. Complete the table. Use your dictionary.**

♂	♀	
father	mother	parents
(dad)	**(1)** (.............)	
uncle	**(2)**	
(3)	sister	
grandfather	**(4)**	grandparents
son	**(5)**	children
(6)	niece	

See Vocabulary Explorer: Page 98

6 **Write the names of six people in your family. Then work in pairs and exchange your lists. Ask and answer questions about three names.**

A: *Who's Susan?*

B: *Susan is my sister. She's five. She's short and fair-haired. She's …*

Grammar: possessive adjectives

7 **Read about Brad and his family again. Complete the table with possessive adjectives.**

Subject pronouns	Possessive adjectives
I	**(1)** ....
you	your
he	his
she	**(2)** ....
it	**(3)** ....
we	our
you	your
they	**(4)** ....

See Grammar Explorer: Page 122

8 **Complete the sentences with possessive adjectives.**

e.g. I'm thirteen and ...my.. brother is fourteen.

1 Jack is tall. .... sister is short.
2 We are English. .... parents are from London.
3 Alice is fair-haired. .... brother is fair-haired too.
4 Martha and Clark are in Antarctica. .... son is in London.
5 This is my cat. .... name is Tiny.
6 Hi, I'm Frank. What's .... name?

Grammar: *this, that, these, those*

9 **Study the examples.**

See Grammar Explorer: Page 122

10 **Complete the sentences with *this, that, these* or *those*.**

1 Hello, Mr Wilson! .... are my sisters, Diana and Lynne.
2 Look! Is .... our teacher in the café?
3 Brad, ... is my friend Meera.
4 Look! Who are .... boys in the park?
5 ....'s my book – give it to me.

Fast finishers

Think of an English word or name for each letter of the alphabet.

Anna, Brad, cat, …

1C Personal information

Reading and listening

1 Look at the photo. Where are Brad and Anna?

2 1.6 **Read and listen to the dialogue. Is Brad happy at the end?**

Librarian:	Are you a member of this library?
Brad:	No, I'm not.
Librarian:	OK. What's your name?
Brad:	Brad Freeman.
Librarian:	How do you spell your surname?
Brad:	F–R–double E–M–A–N.
Librarian:	OK. And what's your address?
Brad:	45 Park Road.
Librarian:	And what's your post code?
Anna:	SE10 9JY.
Librarian:	OK, now what's your telephone number in London?
Brad:	734 0951?
Anna:	Yes, that's right.
Librarian:	Great. And how old are you?
Brad:	I'm fourteen.
Librarian:	OK. This is your Junior Library card.
Brad:	Thanks. Can I borrow this computer game?
Librarian:	Oh dear, I'm sorry. That game is for over sixteens.

3 **Answer the questions about Brad.**

1 What's his surname?
2 What's his address?
3 What's his telephone number?
4 How old is he?
5 Is the game for boys under sixteen?

Listening

4 1.7 **Listen to two more people at the library and complete the sentences.**

1 Her first name is ....
2 His surname is ....
3 Its name is ....
4 His address is 32 .... Road.

5 1.8 **Listen and write the telephone numbers.**

1 734 5221
2 ....
3 ....
4 ....

6 **Write three English names and their telephone numbers. Then work in pairs. Dictate the names and numbers to your partner.**

e.g. John Milton – 0282 567997

Pronunciation: intonation in questions

7 1.9 **Complete these questions from the dialogue. Then listen, check and repeat.**

1 What's y.............. n.............. ?
2 How do you s.............. your s.............. ?
3 What's your a.............. ?
4 What's your p.............. c..............
5 What's your t.............. n.............. ?
6 How .... are y.............. ?

Speaking

8 **Invent a new identity. Then work in pairs. Ask and answer questions. Complete the application form with information about your partner.**

GSC
Greenwich Sports Club

APPLICATION FORM

Name ....
Surname ....
Address ....
Post code ....
Telephone number ....
Age ....

Pronunciation: *is* and *are*

9 1.10 **Listen. Notice that *is* has a very short sound. Repeat.**

Is, is, is, isn't, isn't, isn't.
This is his sister, Liz. Liz is six.
Anna isn't his sister. She isn't six.

10 1.11 **Listen. Notice that *are* has a long sound. Repeat.**

Are, are, are, aren't, aren't, aren't.
Martha and Clark are in Antarctica.

Writing: a form

We use capital letters with:
- days of the week ✔
- months of the year ✔
- names ✔
- addresses ✔

1 **Rewrite the information with capital letters.**

2 **Copy and complete the application form with your information.**

Greenwich Travel Card

Application Form

Name .... brad
Surname .... freeman
Address .... 45 park road,
.... greenwich
Post code se10 9jy
Telephone number 7340951
Age .... fourteen

1D Greenwich: where time begins!

Reading

1 **Look at the photos of Greenwich and read the information. Why is Greenwich special?**

2 **Choose the correct words.**

1 Greenwich is in **New York / London.**
2 It is on the River **Thames / Avon.**
3 It is where world time **begins / ends.**

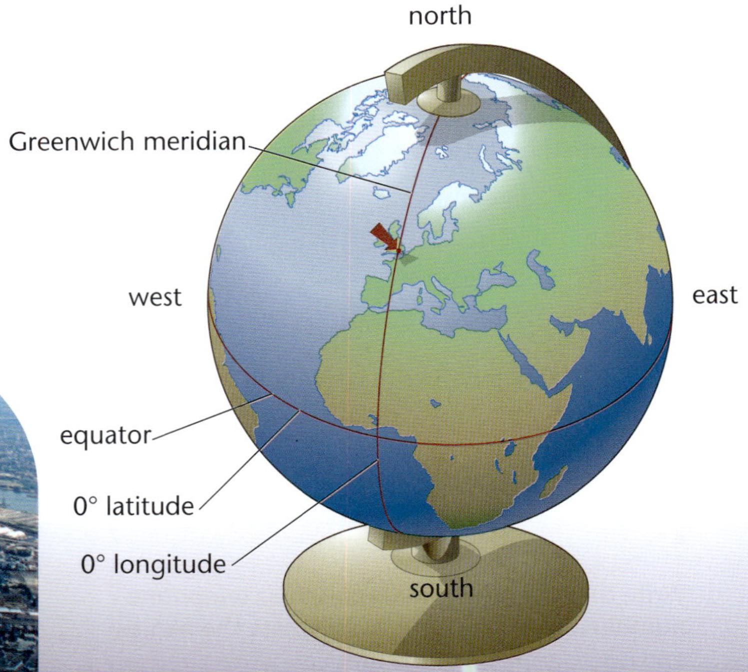

Welcome to Greenwich!

Greenwich is an old historic part of London with green parks and beautiful buildings. It is on the River Thames. Greenwich is also a World Heritage Site. It is a special place in London.

Greenwich is on an imaginary line called the Greenwich meridian. This is where world time begins.

The Greenwich Royal Observatory

Geography and English

Time zones

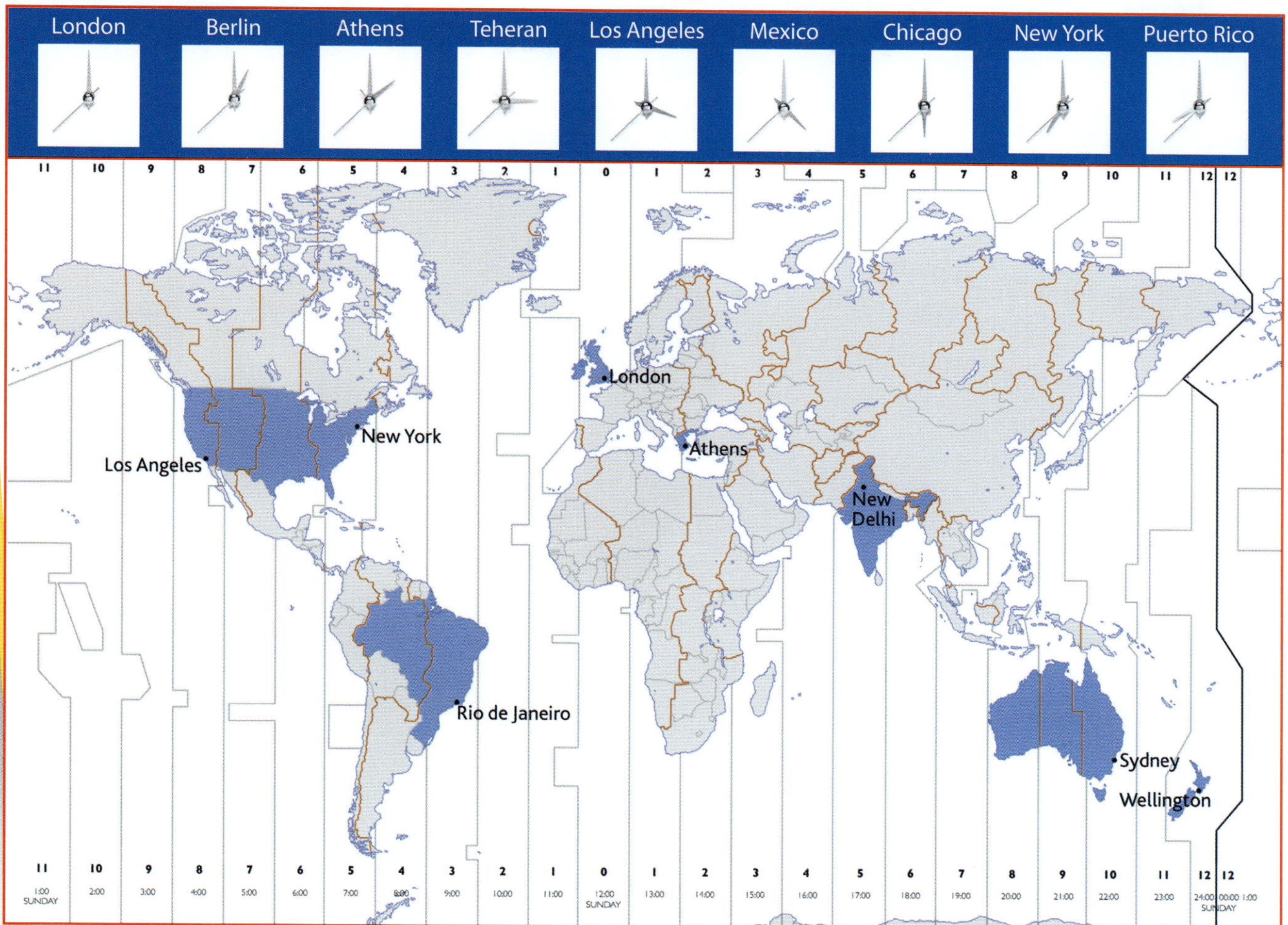

When it's twelve o'clock midnight in London and the UK, it's twelve o'clock midday in New Zealand. New Zealand is east of the Greenwich meridian. Every day, it's morning in New Zealand before it's morning in the UK. The USA is west of the Greenwich meridian. It's morning in the USA after it's morning in the UK.

1 **Look at the map and read the text. How many time zones are there?**

2 **Find the countries on the map.**

Australia **Brazil** **Greece** **India** **New Zealand** **the UK** **the USA**

3 **When it's midnight in London, what time is it in these cities? Match the cities with their times.**

1	New Delhi, India	a	seven o'clock in the evening
2	Wellington, New Zealand	b	ten o'clock in the morning
3	New York, USA	c	four o'clock in the afternoon
4	Rio de Janeiro, Brazil	d	nine o'clock at night
5	Sydney, Australia	e	five o'clock in the morning
6	Athens, Greece	f	midday
7	Los Angeles, USA	g	two o'clock in the morning

1 in the morning
2 in the afternoon
3 in the evening
4 at night

Project

Find out about World Heritage Sites in your country. What are their names? Where are they? Why are they special?

Around the world in a balloon

It's December 1998. Richard Branson, Steve Fosset and Per Lindstrand plan to fly their balloon, The Virgin Challenger, around the world.

1 **Look at the map. Where does the balloon go?**

2 **Read the dialogues. Are the pilots happy at the end of their trip?**

Day 1. Start in Morocco

Richard: Are we ready?
Steve: Yes, we are.
Per: Goodbye! See you soon!
Ground Control: Goodbye!

Day 2. Goodbye, Africa!

R: Where are we now, Per?
P: We're over Egypt.
R: What's our altitude*?
S: 5,000 metres.
R: That's good!

Day 4. Crossing India

S: Wow, look at the Himalayas. They're enormous!
R: Yes, but it's really cold in here.
P: Yes, I'm tired. And hungry! And cold!

Day 6. The Pacific Ocean

P: What's the problem, Steve?
S: Our altitude is low – it's only 2,000 metres.
P: Go up to 4,000 metres.
S: OK, let's try.

Day 7. 15 km from Hawaii

S: Oh no! Our altitude is really low.
P: This is impossible!
S: This is very bad.

*__altitude:__ the height of something in the air

My things

2

> Grammar

Learn about *have got*, the indefinite articles (*a* and *an*), and *can*.

> Vocabulary

Learn words for possessions, and skills and abilities.

> Skills

Read about collections, and about amazing animals.
Listen to teenagers talking about their parents.
Write a thank-you letter.

> Communicate

Make requests, and give dates.

1 Work in pairs. What can you see in the picture?

2 What are your favourite things? What are your partner's favourite things?

3 Write the names of three things:

in your bedroom

in your school bag

See Vocabulary Explorer: Page 100

2A Let's go.

Vocabulary

1 Which of these things can you see in the photo?

a bag	a computer
a key	a mobile
an MP3	a notebook
a pen	a purse
a radio	a travel card
an umbrella	a watch

See Vocabulary Explorer: Page 100

2 Which items in Exercise 1 have you got? Where are they? Write the things in three lists and add two extra items. Use your dictionary.

In my pocket:

In my bag:

At home:

Reading and listening

3 2.1 Read and listen to the dialogue. What's the problem?

Anna: Are you ready, Brad?
Brad: Sure. Let's go. Have you got the invitation to Cool Collections?
Anna: Yes, I have. It's in my bag. Bye, Mum!
Mum: Wait a moment, Anna. Have you got everything?
Anna: Yes, Mum. I've got my key, my purse and my travel card.
Mum: OK. Have you got your mobile?
Anna: Yes, I have.
Mum: And have you got credit on your mobile?
Anna: Oh. No, I haven't.
Mum: Brad, have you got a mobile?
Brad: Well, I've got an American mobile, but I haven't got an English one.
Mum: That's no good. Here, you can borrow my mobile today.
Brad: Thanks, Aunt Jane.
Mum: Now remember, don't be late home.

4 Who has got each item? Complete the sentences.

e.g. *Anna* has got an invitation.

1 .... has got a key.
2 .... has got a travel card.
3 .... has got a purse.
4 .... has got an American mobile.

Grammar: *have got* (affirmative and negative)

5 **Read the dialogue again. Complete the table with short forms.**

Affirmative		
I/You/We/They He/She/It	(**1**) .... (have got) 's got (has got)	a mobile.
Negative		
I/You/We/They He/She/It	(**2**) .... (have got) 's go t (has got)	a mobile.

Don't confuse ***He's*** *American.* (= **He is**) with ***He's got*** *an American mobile.* (= **He has got**)

See Grammar Explorer: Page 122

6 **Write affirmative and negative sentences.**

e.g. Brad has got a mobile.

	Brad	Meera and Harry
	✓	✗
	✗	✓
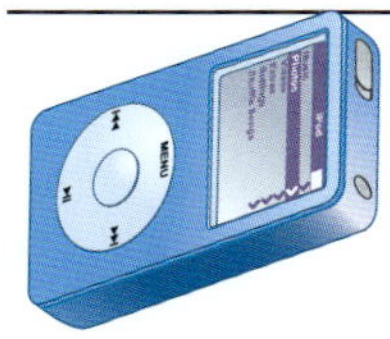	✓	✗
	✓	✓

7 **Write five sentences – four true and one false – about yourself and your family. Then work in pairs and exchange your sentences. Find your partner's false sentence.**

e.g. We've got seven computers in our house.

Grammar: *have got* (questions and short answers)

8 **Read the dialogue again. Complete the table.**

Questions			
(**1**) .... Has	I/you/we/they he/she/it	(**2**) .... got	a key?
Short answers			
Yes,	I/you/we/they he/she/it	(**3**) .... has.	
No,	I/you/we/they he/she/it	(**4**) .... hasn't.	

See Grammar Explorer: Page 123

9 **Write questions with these words.**

e.g. your mum / a purse
Has your mum got a purse?

1. you / a camera?
2. Anna / a bag?
3. you / a dog?
4. Brad / a computer?
5. Anna and Brad / a mobile?
6. you / an umbrella?

10 **Work in pairs. Ask and answer the questions in Exercise 9.**

A: *Has your mum got a purse?*
B: *Yes, she has.*

11 **Use your lists from Exercise 2. Prepare six questions for your partner. Then work in pairs. Ask and answer your questions.**

A: *Have you got a key in your pocket?*
B: *Yes, I have.*
A: *Have you got an umbrella at home?*
B: *No, I haven't.*

Fast finishers

Find six personal items.

C	I	P	P	Q	U	R	T	U	L
K	S	S	Y	E	E	M	P	M	M
B	E	P	E	N	C	I	L	B	A
E	I	Y	I	C	A	M	E	R	A
V	U	Q	T	E	R	M	A	E	O
C	O	M	P	U	T	E	R	L	I
O	J	F	C	I	E	R	B	L	M
X	I	E	B	U	B	A	G	A	R

2B Cool collections

1 ....

I've got about 200 Marvel comics. I've got Spider-man, Captain America and Incredible Hulk comics. My favourite is Spider-man. He can climb buildings and jump across streets. He can't fly – that's Superman! I've got a comic from 1962 – it's very valuable. My valuable comics are in an album.

Harry

2 ....

I've got a collection of fossils. They are really old. I've got an ammonite. It's my favourite. I think the shape is beautiful – it's a spiral, can you see? It's a fossil of an animal. Ammonites and dinosaurs are from the same period. You can find fossils in many places in Britain.

Paula

3 ....

I've got ten toys from my collection here today. This is a model of Indiana Jones, and this is an aeroplane from the first Indiana Jones film. I've got an Orc from *The Lord of the Rings* too. My favourite toy is a car – a James Bond car from 1967. It's very valuable because I've got its original box. That's very important.

David

a

b

c

Reading and listening

1 2.2 Read and listen to the text. Match these headings with the paragraphs. Write the words.

My toys My comics My fossils

2 Read the text again and find their favourite things, a-c.

3 What collections have you got? Work in pairs. Tell your partner about your favourite things.

Grammar: indefinite articles *a* and *an*

4 **Study the table. Then read the text again and find three examples for each group. Add them to the boxes.**

a + singular noun	a comic
an + singular noun starting with a vowel	an album
no article with plural nouns	comics

We use *an* with nouns beginning with *a, e, i, o* and *u* sounds.

See Grammar Explorer: Page 123

5 **Complete the sentences with *a*, *an* or – (no article).**

e.g. I've got ...*an*... umbrella in the car.

1 We've got .... fossil from Australia.
2 She hasn't got .... purse.
3 They've got .... comics from 1950.
4 Harry's got .... album of valuable comics.
5 Paula's got .... ammonites in her collection.
6 I haven't got .... toy train.

Grammar: *can*

6 **Complete the tables with *can* and *can't*.**

Affirmative		
I/you/he/she/it/we/they	(**1**)	build.
Negative		
I/you/he/she/it/we/they	(**2**) .... (cannot)	fly.
Questions		
(**3**)	I/you/he/she/it/we/they	see it?
Short answers		
Yes,	I/you/he/she/it/we/they	can.
No,	I/you/he/she/it/we/they	can't.

See Grammar Explorer: Page 123

7 **Write sentences with *can* and these words. Use *can't* in negative sentences.**

e.g. Spider-man / climb buildings.
Spider-man can climb buildings.

1 Spider-man / not / fly
2 The Incredible Hulk / change colour
3 Orcs / fight
4 Hobbits / not / swim
5 James Bond / drive
6 I / not / drive

8 **Write two true sentences for each picture. Use *I*, *My mum* or *My dad* + *can / can't*.**

e.g. *My dad can't cook pizza. My mum can cook pizza.*

1 cook pizza

2 use a microwave

3 send an email

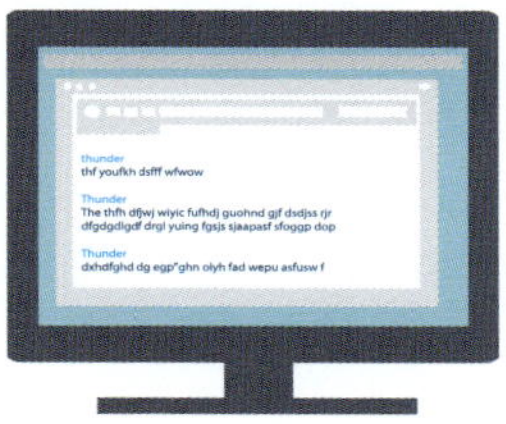

4 use the Internet

5 write text messages

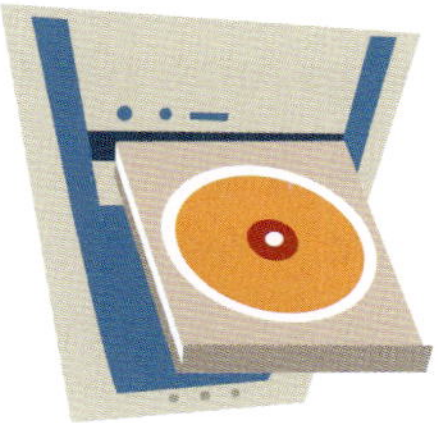

6 copy a CD

Listening

9 2.3 **Listen to three teenagers. Can their parents do the things? (✓ = yes, ✗ = no)**

	Michael's mum	Oscar's dad	Ellie's parents
send emails	✓		
write text messages			
copy CDs			
use a mobile phone			
use the Internet			

10 **Look at the examples and write four true sentences. Use your dictionary.**

I can swim. + I can ski.
= I can swim and ski.

I can't swim. + I can't ski.
= I can't swim or ski.

See Vocabulary Explorer: Page 101

Fast finishers

Look at the photo on page 22 for two minutes. Then close your book. Write down the things you can remember. Look again and check.

2C Requests

Reading and listening

1 2.4 **Read and listen to the dialogue. Find four things Anna asks for.**

Anna: Mum, it's my birthday next month, remember?
Mum: Yes, Anna, I know. It's on the third of November.
Anna: Can I have a new computer?
Mum: Oh, that's expensive! I'm not sure.
Anna: Well, can I have a party at First Light? Please?
Mum: First Light? Is that the new disco in town?
Anna: Yes, it is.
Mum: No! I'm sorry, you can't.
Anna: Well, can I have a party at home?
Mum: Yes, OK. A small party.
Anna: And can you make me an enormous chocolate cake – like last year?
Mum: Yes, of course!
Anna: Thanks, Mum. I love you!

2 Complete the requests with *I*, *you* and *can*.

1 .... have a party at home?
2 .... make me a cake?

3 Write requests with *can* and these words.

e.g. you / help / me?
Can you help me?

1 I / borrow / a pencil?
2 we / have / pizza?
3 I / read / a comic?
4 you / speak slowly?
5 I / use / your dictionary?
6 you / spell / your name?

USEFUL EXPRESSIONS

Can I have pizza?	Can you make me a cake?
No, I'm sorry, you can't.	No, I'm sorry, I can't.
Yes, OK.	Yes, of course.

Pronunciation: stress in questions

4 2.5 **Look at the pictures and write requests. Then listen, check and repeat.**

1 use / mobile

2 borrow / umbrella

3 repeat / name

4 open / window

5 Work in pairs. Make polite requests and responses using the ideas in Exercises 3 and 4.

Vocabulary

6 2.6 **Complete the list of ordinal numbers. Then listen, check and repeat.**

1st	first	**13th**	....
2nd	second	**14th**	....
3rd	third	**15th**	fifteenth
4th	fourth	**16th**	....
5th	fifth	**17th**	....
6th	....	**18th**	....
7th	....	**19th**	....
8th	eighth	**20th**	twentieth
9th	ninth	**21st**	twenty-first
10th	....	**30th**	thirtieth
11th	....	**31st**	thirty-first
12th	twelfth		

We make most ordinal numbers by adding *-th* to the end of the number. Some ordinal numbers are irregular.

7 2.7 **Listen and repeat the dates.**

1/1 14/2 3/3 6/6 22/8 31/10 25/12

We say *the first of January*, but we write *1st January*.

Speaking

8 2.8 **Read and listen to the dialogue. Repeat.**

A: What's your name?
B: My name's Betty.
A: Can you spell that, please?
B: B–E–double T–Y.
A: When's your birthday?
B: It's on the seventh of March.

9 **When is your birthday? How many people in your class have their birthday in the same month? Ask questions and write a list. Use the dialogue in Exercise 8.**

e.g. my birthday – 10th September
Maria – 1st September

Pronunciation: *can* and *can't*

10 2.9 **Listen to these words. Which word has a different sound?**

are aren't can can't

11 2.10 **Listen and repeat.**

1 Can you help me?
2 Yes, I can.
3 Sorry, I can't.
4 I can't speak French.

Writing: a thank-you letter

1 **Complete the thank-you letter with these words.**

band CD great second

2 **Imagine it is your birthday. Write a thank-you letter to your grandmother. Use these ideas.**

1	2	3	4
DVD CD book	lovely fantastic brilliant	actor singer writer	first third fifth

Dear Katy,

Thank you very much for the (1) CD . It's (2) .... Abba's my favourite (3) .... This is the (4) .... CD I've got by Abba.

Love,

Anna

2D Amazing animals

Culture

Reading

1 2.11 Read about pets in the UK. Find the names of the animals in the photos.

2 Answer the questions in the text. Then work in pairs and talk about your answers.

Are pets our best friends?

Fifty-two per cent of families in the UK have got a pet. In fact, British families have got thirteen million cats and dogs! Cats and dogs are typical pets, but some people have got unusual pets too. Birds – for example, parrots – and tropical fish are popular. They are good pets when you haven't got a big house. Some people have got really exotic pets – tortoises and even snakes! Can a snake be your friend?

Some pets can help people too.

Dogs can help blind people and disabled people – they can telephone the emergency services! Some people can't move their arms or legs – monkeys can help in lots of ways. For example, they can operate videos or they can bring food and drinks.

Have you got a pet? Can it do special things? Is your pet your best friend?

a

b

c

g

f

Biology and English

Animal facts

1 **Read the article and answer the question: Are the facts true or false?**

Animals can do things that humans can do – and they can do things that humans can't do. Read these animal facts. Are the facts true or false? Check your answers in the KEY.

1 Tortoises can live over one hundred years.
2 Dogs can recognise hundreds of words.
3 Parrots can count and they can recognise colours.
4 The venom in one bite from King Cobra snakes can kill twenty people.
5 Some tropical fish can change from male to female.
6 Cats can see at night.
7 Monkeys can learn from teachers.

2 **What other things can these animals do? What can't they do?**

Listening

3 2.12 **Listen and complete the table. Then write the names of the animals.**

	legs	tail	wings
1	✗		
2			
3			

Project

What is your favourite animal? Find out about your favourite animal and write a paragraph. Find or draw some pictures of your favourite animal. Make a poster with your paragraph and pictures.

KEY All these facts are true!

Review Units 1 and 2

Vocabulary

1 Complete the family words.

1 brother s.............
2 father m.............
3 uncle a.............
4 son d.............
5 nephew n.............

1 mark per item: .../5 marks

2 Write the opposites.

1 tall ....
2 fair ....
3 sad ....
4 big ....
5 thin ....

1 mark per item: .../5 marks

3 Name the things.

a notebook a watch a camera a purse a mobile phone

1 ....
2 ....
3 ....
4 ....
5 ....

1 mark per item: .../5 marks

4 Complete the sentences with words for animals.

snake fish bird tortoise mouse

1 A .... has got two wings, two legs and a tail.
2 A .... hasn't got legs or wings.
3 A .... has got four legs and a tail.
4 A .... has got a tail. It hasn't got legs, but it can climb.
5 A .... has got four legs and a small tail.

1 mark per item: .../5 marks

5 Write the dates in words.

1 1/9 ....
2 3/5 ....
3 10/10 ....
4 2/12 ....
5 21/2 ....

1 mark per item: .../5 marks

Grammar

6 Complete the sentences with the correct form of *be*.

1 They .... from Australia.
2 .... you hungry?
3 I .... fourteen next week.
4 We .... not cousins.
5 My grandmother .... really old.

1 mark per item: .../5 marks

7 Write sentences with the correct form of *have got*.

1 Mark / a comic (✓)
2 Mark and Jill / bags (✓)
3 Jill / a mobile (✗)
4 Jill / a purse (✓)
5 Mark and Jill / radios (✗)

1 mark per item: .../5 marks

8 Write sentences and questions with *can*.

1 I / not / swim.
2 you / cook?
3 My parents / speak French.
4 your friend / ski?
5 We / not / copy CDs at school.

1 mark per item: .../5 marks

9 Complete the sentences with *a*, *an* or – (no article).

1 Have you got .... umbrella?
2 We can't read .... comics in class.
3 Is it .... album of photos?
4 Paul's got .... collection of model cars.
5 This film is about .... animals in Africa.

1 mark per item: .../5 marks

10 Choose the correct words.

1 This is my sister. **Her / His** name is Jessica.
2 Hi, Kelly! **These / This** are my cousins, Ben and Sam.
3 Can I borrow **my / your** pen, please? Thanks.
4 Look! What are **that / those** birds in that tree?
5 Jack's Australian. **Her / His** parents are from Sydney.

1 mark per item: .../5 marks

Communicate

11 Complete the dialogue with these words.

friends hi meet this welcome

Sam: Hello, Vicky! (**1**) .... to Los Angeles!
Vicky: (**2**) .... , Sam. Thanks.
Sam: Vicky, these are my (**3**) .... Joe and Ross.
Vicky: Nice to (**4**) .... you!
Sam: Joe and Ross, (**5**) .... is my cousin Vicky.
Joe/Ross: Hello!

2 marks per item: .../10 marks

12 Complete the questions.

1. .... your name?
2. .... do you spell your name?
3. .... her address?
4. .... old is he ?
5. .... are you from?

2 marks per item: .../10 marks

13 Choose the correct response.

1. Harry, this is my cousin Brad.
   - a What's your name?
   - b Hi, who is it?
   - c Nice to meet you!
2. How old are you?
   - a On the third of March.
   - b I'm thirteen next month.
   - c Yes, my grandfather's seventy.
3. What's your telephone number?
   - a Yes, I have.
   - b It's 936 5845.
   - c DL15 9NT.
4. Can I borrow your phone?
   - a No, I'm sorry.
   - b No, thanks.
   - c Yes, I can.
5. Can you make a pizza?
   - a No, you can't.
   - b Yes, I am.
   - c Yes, of course.

2 marks per item: .../10 marks

14 Write the plural form of the words.

1. box ....
2. toy ....
3. glass ....
4. library ....
5. umbrella ....
6. party ....
7. key ....
8. watch ....
9. phone ....
10. potato ....

1 mark per item: .../10 marks

15 Rewrite the information in the thank-you letter with capital letters.

58 london road
tonbridge
kent
tn6 8pj
6th january

dear andrew and sam,

thank you very much for the cd. it's fantastic. metallica's my favourite band. the poster is great too.

thanks again,

josh

½ mark per item: .../10 marks

Total: .../100

I can...

I can make introductions
I can give personal information.
I can make requests.
I can give dates.

PROJECT

Business card collector

Reading

Read the article and answer the questions.

My collection

By Philip Daniel, Denver, Colorado, USA

Getting started

I collect business cards. It's easy to collect them. You can get business cards in shops or offices. Ask your family and friends - they can give you some. You can collect cards on holiday too. My friend is from Peru and sometimes she gives me some from South America.

1 What does Philip collect?
2 Is it difficult?
3 How can you find business cards?
4 Where is Philip's friend from?

What do you do?

Collect the cards you like. Some people like cards with different colours. My favourite cards have got pictures on them. I've got about 200 cards but some people have got over 50,000!

Buy an album. I've got two albums now. I've got a business card with my name and address on it too. I give it to people and they sometimes send me cards (I always send a thank-you letter or email).

5 What have Philip's favourite cards got?
6 How many cards has he got?
7 What do you need to buy?
8 Why does Philip have a card with his name and address on it?

Why I like it

It's interesting – and you don't need a lot of money. I've got cards from Africa, Europe and Australia. They are not very old or valuable, but that's OK – I do it for fun!

9 Do you need a lot of money to collect ca
10 Why does Philip do it?

Project

Have you got a collection? Have you got lots of stamps, coins, photographs, songs or magazines? Write an article. Say:

- How you get started
- What you do
- Why you like it
- Find pictures for your article on the Internet or in magazines

NATIONAL GEOGRAPHIC

3 My interests

> Grammar

Learn about the present simple, the definite article - *the*, and object pronouns.

> Vocabulary

Learn words for school subjects, interests and activities, and food.

> Skills

Read about famous people and their interests, and about food in the UK.

Listen to instructions.

Write an email.

> Communicate

Talk about your favourite activities, and order a meal.

1 How do you think the people in the picture feel?

2 3.1 Listen. What's the conversation about?

a fashion b film c music

3 Write a list of your favourite people and things.

actors films sports books food singers

See Vocabulary Explorer: Pages 102–103

4 Work in pairs and compare your lists. What have you got in common?

3A I love it!

Reading and listening

1 3.2 **Read and listen to the emails from two French students. Choose the correct words.**

e.g. Marie loves **cars** / **animals**.

1. Marie likes **physics** / **fashion**.
2. Marie hates **sports** / **tennis**.
3. Chantal likes **motorbikes** / **rap**.
4. Chantal loves **snakes** / **Formula 1**.
5. Chantal doesn't like **pizza** / **school**.

a

Hi!
My name's Marie. I'm thirteen years old. At school, I like art and music (I can play the guitar a bit) but I don't like physics or IT. They are really boring and difficult. I like fashion and shopping. My favourite film star is Orlando Bloom. I love him! I've got all his films on DVD. I hate sports, except tennis. I love Roger Federer! I love animals too – I've got five hamsters, two cats and a dog. My dog doesn't like my cats!
Have you got similar interests to me? Write to me at marie01@lycee.org.fr

b

Hello!
I'm Chantal. I'm 13 next month. I've got a brother and a sister. They are 14 and 16. We all like motorbikes and cars and my brother loves Formula 1. I love snakes – I've got three in a tank at home. I can speak English and Italian (I like pizza, too!). I like languages but I don't like history, geography or biology. Actually, I don't like school! My favourite music is heavy metal and I hate rap.
Have you got similar interests to me? Write to me at chantal22@lycee.org.fr

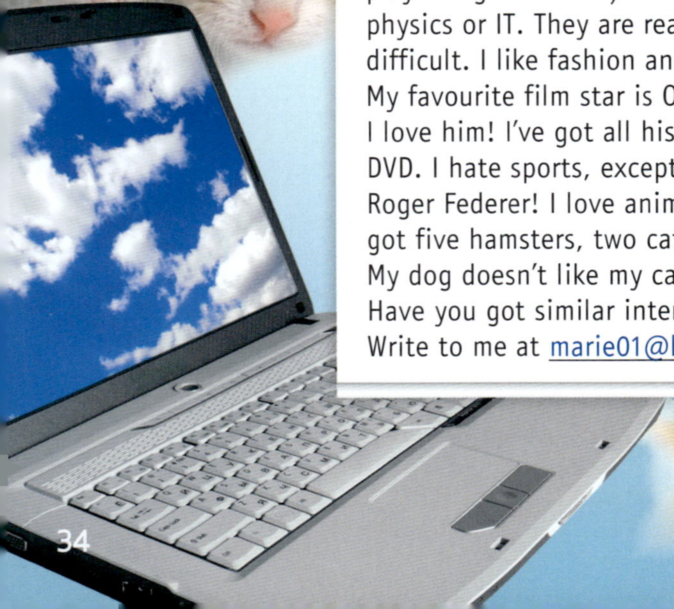

Vocabulary

2 **Read the emails again and find nine school subjects. What subjects are missing?**

See Vocabulary Explorer: Page 102

3 **Make two lists of school subjects: *I like / I don't like …* . Then work in pairs and compare your lists.**

4 3.3 **Listen. What's the conversation about?**

a history
b geography
c music

Grammar: present simple (affirmative and negative)

5 **Read the emails and the sentences in Exercise 1 again. Complete the table.**

Affirmative		
I/You/We/They He/She/It	(1) .... (2)	art.
Negative		
I/You/We/They He/She/It	(3) .... like (do not like) (4) .... like (does not like)	IT.

The main verb (*like*) does not change in the negative form – we don't add *-s* or *-es*.

See Grammar Explorer: Page 123

6 **Write sentences with these words. Use short forms in negative sentences.**

e.g. I / like / dogs
I like dogs.

1 we / not like / spiders
2 she / hate / physics
3 they / love / IT
4 David / not like / fashion
5 you / not like / pizza
6 Brad / like / sports

7 **Look at the table. Write sentences.**

e.g. Harry hates fashion.

	Harry	**Anna and Meera**
fashion	😠	😀
films	😀	🙂
comics	😀	😑
sports	😠	😑
animals	😑	🙂

KEY 😀 = love, 😠 = hate, 🙂 = like, 😑 = not / like

8 **Work in pairs. Which activities do you like, love or hate? Tell your partner.**

e.g. *I like cooking.*

cooking **cycling** **dancing** **drawing** **painting**
reading **shopping** **singing** **sleeping** **swimming**

See Vocabulary Explorer: Page 102

After *like, love* and *hate*, we can use nouns or *-ing* words.

See Grammar Explorer: Page 124

9 **Choose four activities. Think of a friend or somebody in your family for each activity. Work in pairs. Tell your partner.**

e.g. *My friend Sam doesn't like reading.*

Fast finishers

Find the odd word out in each list. Then write more lists for a partner.

1 snake hamster guitar fish
2 teacher friend brother sport
3 biology IT maths TV
4 basketball school tennis golf
5 chocolate cycling shopping sleeping

3B Celebrity secrets

Reading and listening

1 3.4 Read and listen to the text. Who are the people? Why are they famous?

Celebrity secrets

*Can you guess the **secret interests** of these stars?*

The films of Peter Jackson are very popular. He is the director of *The Lord of the Rings* and *King Kong*. The original 1933 film of *King Kong* is his favourite film. Peter's from New Zealand and he's married. He's got two children.

Kate Moss is a very popular fashion model. She's from London and she isn't married. She's got one daughter. One of her best friends is Stella McCartney, the fashion designer. Kate is a designer too. You can buy the Kate Moss collections at Topshop, the famous UK clothes shop.

Andy Serkis is the actor 'inside' King Kong. He's Gollum in *The Lord of the Rings* too. The voice of Gollum is copied from his cat! Andy's from London. He and his wife have got a house and a studio there. Andy loves painting and playing with his children.

Secret interests:

1 I love climbing mountains.
2 I don't like meat – I'm a vegetarian.
3 I like collecting model aeroplanes.
4 I like wearing shorts.
5 I love rock music. My ambition is to be a rock star.
6 I like pop music from the 1960s.

Listening

2 3.5 **Work in pairs. Match the secret interests with the people. Then listen and check.**

See Vocabulary Explorer: Page 102

Grammar: definite article *the*

3 Look at the sentences from the text. Notice how we use *the* with singular and plural nouns. Find five more examples in the text.

The films of Peter Jackson are very popular. He is the director of *The Lord of the Rings*.

See Grammar Explorer: Page 124

4 Circle the correct words.

Peter Jackson's *King Kong* is (**1**) the third / third film of *King Kong*. It's a great adventure story. (**2**) The film / Film is about a giant ape on an island in (**3**) the Pacific Ocean / Pacific Ocean. (**4**) The main actors / Main actors are Jack Black and Naomi Watts.

5 3.6 **Andy Serkis is King Kong and Peter Jackson is the director. Peter is giving instructions to Andy. Put the instructions in order. Then listen and check.**

a Don't look at the camera. Good.
b Action! Look at me.
c Touch her on her arm.
d Eat it. That's right. Now stand up. Look at the policeman.
e Don't smile at him. Go to the girl.
f And … cut!
g Don't look at it. OK, Andy. Find the bananas.
h Very good. Look at them now. Take a banana.

Grammar: object pronouns

6 Read the instructions in Exercise 5 again. Match the underlined words with the words they refer to.

1 Look at me.	**a** the bananas
2 Eat it.	**b** the banana
3 Touch her.	**c** the director
4 Look at them now.	**d** the policeman
5 Don't smile at him.	**e** the girl

See Grammar Explorer: Page 124

7 Complete the table with the underlined words from Exercise 7.

Subject pronouns	Object pronouns
I	(**1**) ....
you	you
he	(**2**) ....
she	(**3**) ....
it	(**4**) ....
we	us
you	you
they	(**5**) ....

See Grammar Explorer: Page 124

8 Complete the sentences with object pronouns.

e.g. You're my friend. I like ..you...

1 I'm the director. Listen to ....
2 Peter Jackson likes model aeroplanes. He likes collecting ....
3 Naomi Watts is his favourite actress. He loves ....
4 We've got the map. Follow ....
5 Kate Moss doesn't like meat. She hates ....
6 Andy Serkis is fantastic. I like ....

Fast finishers

Put the letters in the correct order to make words. Write true sentences with *like, love* and *hate*.

libicngm stnelveiio shfanio orspts inrdeag ooslch

3C Eating out

Vocabulary

1 **Match the things on the menu with the pictures.**

e.g. beefburger – d

See Vocabulary Explorer, Page 103

2 **Work in pairs. Look at the menu again. Which food is healthy? Which food do you like?**

Reading and listening

3 3.7 **Listen and tick (✓) the food that Anna, Brad, Harry and Meera order on the menu. Then read the dialogue and check your answers.**

Assistant:	Good afternoon. Can I help you?
Brad:	Yeah. Can I have a double cheeseburger and chips, please?
Assistant:	Of course.
Anna:	A double cheeseburger! Brad!
Brad:	Yes, I'm hungry! And large chips, please.
Assistant:	And for you?
Meera:	Well, we don't like meat.
Assistant:	We've got vegetarian burgers.
Harry:	Good, we'd like two, please.
Anna:	And I'd like a beefburger.
Assistant:	The double or the triple burger?
Anna:	Triple burger??!! No, thanks! A single burger – and a green salad.
Brad:	And four milkshakes – chocolate milkshakes, please.
Assistant:	Here you are.
Brad:	Thanks. How much is that?
Assistant:	That's thirteen pounds fifty, please.
Brad:	Here you are.

4 3.8 **Listen and repeat the *Useful expressions*.**

USEFUL EXPRESSIONS

Can I help you?
Can I have a burger, please?
I'd like a drink, please.
We'd like two milkshakes, please.
How much is that?
Here you are.

Speaking

5 **Work in pairs. Look at the menu again and prepare a similar dialogue in a restaurant.**

Pronunciation

6 3.9 **These words have a *th* sound. Listen and repeat.**

that they the this brother
mother clothes

3.10 **These words have a *t* sound at the end. Listen and repeat.**

cat art meat hate that
right eight late

7 3.11 **Practise these sentences.**

That cat hates the meat I give it to eat.
This is my father and that's my mother.
I've got three sisters and one big brother.

Writing: an email

1 **Rewrite the email using short forms.**

e.g. My name's Jamie.

2 **Match the sentences in Exercise 1 with these headings.**

- a My favourite things
- b Age
- c Name
- d Likes and dislikes
- e Family

3 **Write notes about yourself for the headings (a–e) in Exercise 2.**

4 **Write a reply to one of the emails on page 34. Begin *Dear …* and end with your name.**

Dear Jacques,
Hi! My name is Jamie. I am twelve. I have got a brother. I do not like animals. My favourite school subject is maths.

Best wishes,

Jamie

3D Food in the UK

Reading and listening

1 Look at the photos. Can you name the food items?

2 3.12 **Read and listen. Match the numbers in the text with the photos.**

Culture

In the UK people like eating traditional British food and they love international food too. The traditional 'fast food' is (**1**) *fish and chips.* In the summer, (**2**) *strawberries* are traditional, and it's a great time to eat (**3**) *fresh salad* too. British people love (**4**) *cakes* all year!

Indian food is popular in the UK. You can eat (**5**) *curry* with special bread and have a delicious (**6**) *yoghurt drink*. Lots of vegetarians also like eating Indian food.

The British love eating (**7**) *Chinese food* too. It's difficult to eat with chopsticks but people like trying!

One food that everyone loves, of course, is (**8**) *ice cream*!

a

b

c

d

e

f

g

h

Listening

3 3.13 **Listen to Rosa and her friends. Match the countries with the food items and dishes.**

1	Spain	a	chocolate
2	Italy	b	paella
3	France	c	pasta
4	Belgium	d	pâté

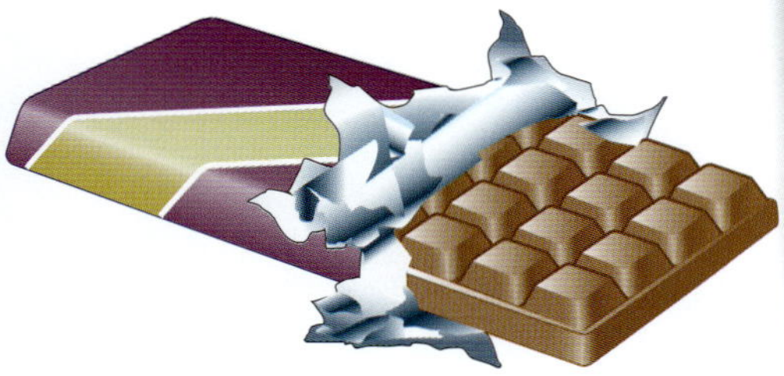

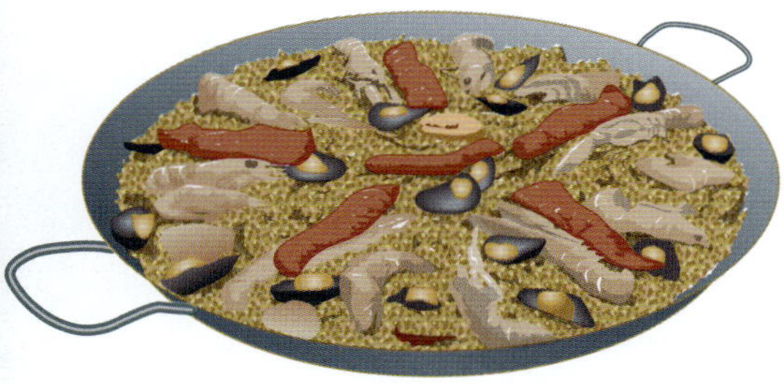

4 **Work in pairs. Choose two typical dishes from your country. What are the ingredients? Use a dictionary.**

Biology and English

A balanced diet

1 **What is a balanced diet? Read and find out.**

What is a balanced diet?
A balanced diet includes food from different groups. Look at the diagram. Can you name each food?

Why is it important?
Your body isn't healthy without food from each group.

How can I have a balanced diet?
Eat food from each group every day. Eat lots from groups 1 and 2. Don't eat too much from groups 3 and 4.

2 **Look at the diagram again and find food in the photos on this page for each group. Can you make a balanced meal with traditional British food?**

Project

What do you eat? In a notebook write the food you eat for breakfast, lunch and dinner for one week.

Find pictures and make a poster of your diet.

Do you have a balanced diet? Make a poster of a balanced diet.

Yuri Gagarin – the first man in space

TRUE STORY

1 **Read the story of Yuri Gagarin. Are these sentences true or false?**

1	Yuri isn't a good student at school.	T / F
2	Yuri and his wife have two children.	T / F
3	Yuri doesn't like flying.	T / F
4	Yuri wants to be the first man in space.	T / F
5	Vostok 1 goes around the moon at 27,000 kilometres per hour.	T / F
6	Yuri dies when he is an old man.	T / F

2 **Read the story again and say why these dates are important.**

November 1957
March 1968
March 1934
April 1961

1 Yuri is born not far from Moscow in March 1934.

2 Yuri's parents work on a farm. His mother, Anna, likes reading and his father, Alexey, enjoys making things out of wood.

3 At school, Yuri's favourite subject is mathematics, and he also learns physics and science. He becomes interested in space and the planets. He loves flying and really wants to go into space one day.

4 Yuri learns to fly small aeroplanes. In November 1957, he becomes a pilot and he marries Valentina Goryacheva. They have two children together.

5 Yuri works hard because he wants to be the first man in space. He also likes relaxing and he loves swimming, fishing and camping with friends.

6 In April 1961 becomes the first man in space. In his spacecraft, Vostok 1, he goes around the earth at 27,000 kilometres per hour!

7 Yuri Gagarin is now famous! He travels to Italy, Britain and Japan with his wife. But he isn't happy travelling around the world – he wants to go into space again!

8 Sadly, Yuri does not go into space again. In March 1968, he dies in an aeroplane crash. He is only 34 years old. Today, there is a town in Russia and a place on the moon with the name Gagarin, and we remember him as the first true space explorer!

NATIONAL GEOGRAPHIC

My day

4

> Grammar

Learn about the present simple, question words, and adverbs of frequency.

> Vocabulary

Learn words for sports, and daily routine.

> Skills

Read about circus performers, and about Olympic athletes.

Listen to an interview.

Write a report.

> Communicate

Talk about your daily routine.

1 **Look at the picture. When is time important?**

2 4.1 **Listen. Choose the three sports you hear.**

athletics cycling football
Formula 1 swimming tennis

See Vocabulary Explorer: Page 104

3 **Write two things you do:**

after school

at the weekend

at the same time every day

4 **Work in pairs and compare your lists. What have you got in common?**

4A Do you like sports?

Reading and listening

1 4.2 **Read and listen to the dialogue. When is the football match?**

Harry: Hey, Brad. I really like playing basketball.
Brad: Yeah, and you're really great!
Harry: Thanks! Do you like football?
Brad: Yes, I do. I like playing and watching.
Harry: Good, because my dad's got three tickets for the match on Saturday.
Brad: Great!
Harry: It starts at 3.00 pm.
Brad: OK. What time does it finish?
Harry: About 5.00 pm. Hey, Brad! It's English football, you know.
Brad: Of course! I know you don't play American football here.
Harry: OK, sorry! Anyway, it's Chelsea against Manchester United.
Brad: Does your dad go to the match every Saturday?
Harry: Yes, he does. He loves Chelsea!
Brad: OK, then. See you on Saturday.

2 **Choose the correct words.**

1 Brad **likes / doesn't like** football.
2 The game **starts / finishes** at 5.00 pm.
3 Harry's dad **plays / watches** football every Saturday.

Vocabulary

3 Match these sports with the pictures. Are these sports popular in your country?

a

b

c

d

e

f

g

h

i

j

athletics basketball boxing football
gymnastics hockey skating skiing
swimming tennis

See Vocabulary Explorer: Page 104

Grammar: present simple (questions and short answers)

4 Read the dialogue again. Complete the tables.

Questions			
(1) .... (2)	I/you/we/they he/she/it	like go	football? to the match?
Short answers			
Yes,	I/you/we/they he/she/it	(3) .... (4)	
No,	I/you/we/they he/she/it	don't doesn't	

The main verb does not change in questions – we don't add *-s* or *-es*.

See Grammar Explorer: Page 124

5 Complete the questions with *do* or *does*. Then write short answers.

e.g. Does Brad like football? (✓) Yes, he does.

1 .... Harry support Chelsea? (✓)
2 .... you play tennis? (✗)
3 .... Anna love skating? (✓)
4 .... they go to every match? (✗)
5 .... Jane go swimming on Saturdays? (✗)
6 .... we go to school on Mondays? (✓)

6 Write six questions with the words in the box. Then ask your partner.

Do Does	you your parents your best friend your teacher	go like live play speak support	al sports team? computer games? French? in your street? to football matches? volleyball?

Grammar: questions with *Wh-* words

7 Read the dialogue again. Complete the table.

Questions with *Wh-* words			
What What time	(1) .... (2)	I/you/we/they he/she/it	mean? finish?

See Grammar Explorer: Page 124

8 4.3 **Match the questions (1–4) with the answers (a–d). Then listen and check.**

1 What time does the race start? b
2 When do you play tennis?
3 Where does your friend live?
4 What do you want for your birthday?

a In Sun Street.
b At 10.00 a.m.
c Every Sunday.
d A new bike.

9 Write questions for these answers.

e.g. Anna goes skating every weekend. (When)
When does Anna go skating?

1 Martha lives in Los Angeles. (Where)
2 I like chicken on pizza. (What)
3 The film finishes at 8.00 pm. (What time)
4 They watch the match on TV. (Where)

Fast finishers

Find five pairs of verbs. Write a sentence with each verb.

drea keaps nishfi teha tenlsi
itwre yalp ttars vole wkro

4B At the circus

Reading and listening

1 4.4 **Look at the photos and listen to the first part of an interview with Zhang Jin, a circus performer. Does she perform on her own or in a group?**

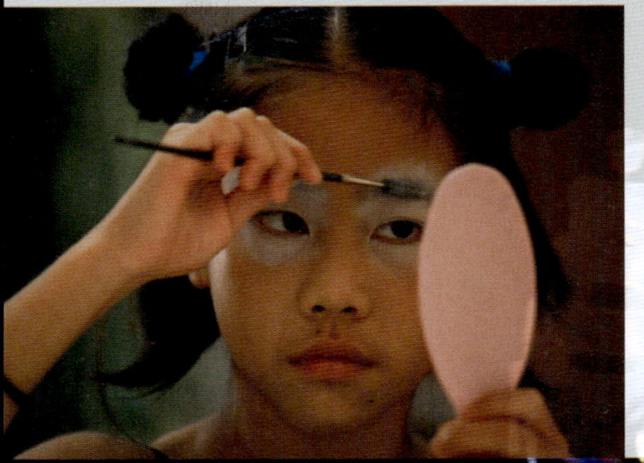

2 4.4 **Complete the interview with these verbs. Then listen again and check.**

do	**get**	**go**	**practise**	**prepares**	**train**	~~**wake up**~~

Zhang Jin: My name is Zhang Jin. I'm from Beijing in China and I'm eleven years old.

Interviewer: Zhang Jin, tell us about your life.

Zhang Jin: Well, some kids (**1**) wake up every day and go to school. I wake up and (**2**) .... to the circus. I (**3**) .... an act with my best friends called *Diabolicos* in the Cirque du Soleil. I love it. We usually do ten shows every week. The preparation is hard. We run every morning with our coach, then we (**4**) .... for two hours. We (**5**) .... jumping, balancing and spinning. In the evenings, we (**6**) .... ready for the shows. Our coach (**7**) .... our costumes but I always do my own make up.

3 4.5 **Match the questions (1–5) with the answers (a–e). Then listen to the end of the interview and check.**

1 Where does the Cirque du Soleil perform? d
2 Where do you live now?
3 Are you tired after a show?
4 Does it hurt?
5 What do you do in your free time?

a In the USA but my family lives in China.
b No, I'm never tired. Working in the Cirque du Soleil gives me energy.
c It sometimes hurts but my body's very flexible.
d We usually perform in Florida, in the USA.
e I do normal things. I often go to the beach but I sometimes study.

Grammar: adverbs of frequency

4 **Complete the sentences with words from the interview in Exercises 2 and 3.**

100% **e.g.** I always do my own make up.
1 We .... do ten shows every week.
2 I .... go to the beach.
3 It .... hurts.
0% 4 I'm .... tired.

Adverbs of frequency go before main verbs but after *be*.

See Grammar Explorer: Page 124

5 **Put the words in order to make sentences.**

e.g. for two hours / the team / trains / always / on Saturdays
The team always trains for two hours on Saturdays.

1 at weekends / never / my friend / studies
2 an email / Zhang Jin / sometimes / her parents / sends
3 often / my best friend and I / Chinese / speak
4 at weekends / usually / get ready early / we / for the show

Listening

6 4.6 **Listen to four more people from the Cirque du Soleil. Match the people (1–4) with their jobs (a–d).**

1	Gisela	a	acrobat
2	Lee	b	clown
3	Joseph	c	coach
4	Tanya	d	dancer

7 4.6 **Listen again. Who does each activity? Write sentences with adverbs of frequency.**

e.g. Gisela / usually
b Gisela usually goes to the gym.

1	Lee / always	a	go swimming
2	he / sometimes	b	go to the gym
3	Joseph / always	c	run
4	he / often	d	play golf
5	Tanya / sometimes	e	cycle
6	she / usually	f	go to the cinema
		g	do exercises

8 **Complete the sentences about your free-time activities. Use the adverbs of frequency.**

e.g. After school, I usually go swimming.

After school, I …
At weekends, I …
In the holidays, I …

Fast finishers

Work in pairs. Write sentences about what your partner does in the evening. Use adverbs of frequency.

go to a football match
visit relatives
listen to a CD
watch TV
do homework

4C Daily routines

Reading and listening

1 4.7 **Read and listen to the dialogue. What's the problem?**

Teacher: What time is it, Harry?
Harry: It's five past nine, sir.
Teacher: And what time does school start?
Harry: At five to nine, sir.
Teacher: What time do you get up, Harry?
Harry: Well, sir, my alarm clock goes off at twenty to eight.
Teacher: But what time do you get up?
Harry: I sometimes get up at ... twenty past eight.
Teacher: Why do you get up late?
Harry: I don't know, sir. I don't hear my alarm clock.
Teacher: What do you do in the evening? Do you play computer games all night?
Harry: No, sir, I don't. I watch TV and I do my homework.
Teacher: Do you go to bed late?
Harry: No, sir. I usually go to bed at ten to ten.
Teacher: Well, Harry. You're late again. That's the third time this week, and today's Wednesday. It's lunchtime detention for you until Friday.
Harry: Yes, sir.

2 **Answer the questions.**

1 What time does school start?
2 What time does Harry get up?
3 What does he do in the evenings?
4 What time does he go to bed?

Vocabulary

3 **What time do you do these things? Put the activities in the correct order and add a time.**

e.g. I get up – 7.20

arrive home	do my homework	get dressed
get up	go to bed	have a bath/shower
have dinner	leave the house	

See Vocabulary Explorer: Page 105

Speaking

4 **Work in pairs. Ask and answer questions about the activities in Exercise 3. Write the answers.**

e.g. **A:** *What time do you get up?*
B: *At twenty past seven.*
I get up at 7.20 (me) – 7.20 (my partner)

5 **Find out three more activities your partner does every day.**

e.g. **A:** *Do you play computer games every day?*
B: *Yes, I do. / No, I don't.*

6 **Write three sentences about things you and your partner both do.**

e.g. We both get up at 7.20.

Pronunciation: words with /ɜː/

7 4.8 **Listen to these words. Notice that they all have the same sound. Repeat.**

burger	circus	first	girl	her	hurt	learn
purse	third	turn	work	world		

8 4.9 **Listen and repeat these sentences. Can you say them quickly?**

1 The girl in the circus likes burgers.
2 It's her turn to learn the third word.

Writing: a report

1 **Match pairs of sentences. Then rewrite the sentences with *and* or *but*.**

e.g. I like football, but I don't like tennis.

1 I like football. b
2 She lives in London.
3 We eat salad every day.
4 I leave school at 4.00 pm.
5 I support Manchester United.

a I get home at 4.25.
b I don't like tennis.
c She's got two cats.
d I don't go to their matches.
e My dad never eats healthy food.

2 **Complete the report with *and* or *but*.**

3 **Write a report about daily routines. Use the information from Exercises 4 and 5, and write about you and your partner. Use *and*, *but* or *both*. Begin like this.**

e.g. ... and I are very similar / different.

Report: routines in our family

In the morning, I get up at 07.30 (1) .... I have a shower. I have cereal for breakfast (2) .... my brother doesn't like cereal. I leave the house at 8.35 (3) .... I get to school at 8.55. I'm never late for school (4) .... my brother is often late. In the evening, we have our dinner (5) .... we do our homework. My brother watches TV (6) .... I hate TV. I read comics. We both go to bed at 10.15.

4D Olympic athletes

Culture

Reading

1 What do you know about the Olympic Games? Work in pairs and do this quiz. Check your answers in the KEY.

1 The Olympic Games are every … years.
a two **b** four **c** ten

2 The Games are in the
a summer. **b** winter. **c** winter and summer.

3 About … people compete in the Games.
a 1,300 **b** 13,000 **c** 130,000

4 The Paralympic Games are for … athletes.
a professional **b** young **c** disabled

5 Olympic athletes compete in … different sports.
a 17 **b** 35 **c** 59

6 About … million people watch the Games.
a 1.2 **b** 4.7 **c** 20

7 The Olympic logo represents
a five areas of sport. **b** the five continents. **c** 500 years of Olympic Games.

8 The Olympic Games originally come from
a Greece. **b** Rome. **c** Asia.

Listening

2 **4.10 Listen to a radio programme about Tom Daley, an Olympic diver. Are the sentences true or false?**

1. Tom is a teenager. **T / F**
2. He's from America. **T / F**
3. He has got some medals for diving. **T / F**
4. Leon Taylor and Lance Armstrong are his friends. **T / F**
5. He wants to win a medal in London. **T / F**

Reading and listening

3 **4.11 Read and listen to different opinions about young Olympic athletes. Who do you agree with?**

What do you think?

Young athletes make lots of sacrifices to compete in the Olympics. Is this good or bad?

I think it's bad. They train all the time and they can't have fun with their friends.

Kim, 12, Manchester

It's good, it's great, it's an opportunity. Lots of things in life are difficult.

Andrea, 12, Belfast

The Olympics are a fantastic dream! Can you imagine winning a medal? Go for it!

Brent, 13, Los Angeles

You can hurt yourself in competitions and training. You can break your legs or your arms. It's not good for young people.

Ellis, 11, Sydney

Maths and English

Statistics

1 **Look at the medal table for the 2008 Olympic Games. Work out the missing numbers and complete the table.**

Olympic Games 2008 total medal table

	country	Gold	Silver	Bronze	total
1	China	**(1)**	21	28	100
2	USA	36	38	36	**(2)** ....
3	Russia	23	21	**(3)**	72
4	Great Britain	**(4)**	13	15	47
5	Germany	16	**(5)**	15	41
6	Australia	14	15	17	**(6)** ....
81	Venezuela	0	0	1	1
	total	302	303	353	958

2 **The total number of medals is 958. What is the percentage of gold medals?**

- **a** about 25%
- **b** about 33%
- **c** about 50%

3 **The total number of countries in the games is 204. 81 have got medals. What percentage is that?**

- **a** about 20%
- **b** about 40%
- **c** about 60%

4 **The total number of athletes is 11,658. What percentage have got medals?**

- **a** about 8%
- **b** about 38%
- **c** about 80%

4 **Which of these sports are popular in your country? Write the names of sports people for two sports. Work in pairs and compare the names.**

athletics basketball cycling
football Formula 1 tennis

Project

Choose one of your sports heroes. Find out about their sports career and find an interesting photo. Prepare a presentation for the class about your hero.

KEY **1** b **2** c **3** b **4** c **5** b **6** b **7** b **8** 8

Review Units 3 and 4

Vocabulary

1 Complete the school timetable.

	Mon	Tues	Wed
9.00	(**1**) b............	(**3**) a............	(**4**) g............
9.45			English
10.30	BREAK		
10.45	(**2**) h............	IT	(**5**) p............

1 mark per item: .../5 marks

2 Write the interests.

1. I like d............ pictures.
2. I can sing and play the guitar. I like m............ .
3. I like r............ books and comics.
4. I get up late on Sundays. I like s............ .
5. I like f............ . I go to the cinema every week.

1 mark per item: .../5 marks

3 Write the food items.

1. ....
2. ....
3. ....
4. ....
5. ....

1 mark per item: .../5 marks

4 Write the sports and games.

1. a sport in water: s............
2. a summer game for 2 or 4 people: t............
3. a race in cars: F............
4. Liverpool has a great team: f............
5. a team game for tall people: b............

1 mark per item: .../5 marks

5 Complete the sentences with five of these verbs.

arrive eat get up go leave play start watch

1. I .... at 7.00 a.m. every morning.
2. I .... the house after breakfast.
3. I .... to school on the bus.
4. I .... football after school.
5. I .... TV in the evenings.

1 mark per item: .../5 marks

Grammar

6 Complete the sentences with the correct form of the verbs.

1. They .... in London. (**live**)
2. We .... gymnastics. (**not / like**)
3. She .... physics and maths. (**hate**)
4. He .... to my school. (**not / go**)
5. My brother .... every day. (**train**)

1 mark per item: .../5 marks

7 Complete the questions and answers.

1. .... your brother get up at 7.00 a.m.? Yes, ...
2. .... Mark and Jill go to school on Sundays? No, ...
3. .... you like maths? Yes, ...
4. .... your sister listen to the radio? No, ...
5. .... your teachers give lots of homework? Yes, ...

1 mark per item: .../5 marks

8 Choose the correct words.

1. We **sometimes go / go sometimes** to the circus.
2. My dad **often is / is often** tired.
3. I **have always / always have** eggs for breakfast.
4. Ben **usually gets / gets usually** home at 4.30.
5. I **never am / am never** late in the morning.

1 mark per item: .../5 marks

9 Replace the underlined words with the correct object pronouns.

1. Look at the people. ....
2. I love my sister. ....
3. Give the DVD to the boy. ....
4. My mum doesn't like the film. ....
5. I don't like those comics. ....

1 mark per item: .../5 marks

10 Complete the questions with these words.

what what time where why when

1. .... do you live?
2. .... is your birthday?
3. .... do you usually do after school?
4. .... is lunch? 1.00 p.m. or 2.00 p.m.?
5. .... is she always late for school?

1 mark per item: .../5 marks

Communicate

11 Complete the dialogue with the sentences.

OK, and for you? | Good afternoon. Can I help you? | Here you are. | That's six pounds forty, please. | Thank you.

Assistant: (**1**) ....
Sam: Yes, can we have two burgers, please?
Assistant: (**2**) ....
Ross: Thanks. I'd like a chocolate milkshake too.
Assistant: (**3**) ....
Sam: A can of cola, please.
Assistant: (**4**) ....
Ross: OK. Here you are.
Assistant: (**5**) ....
Ross: Thanks.

2 marks per item: .../10 marks

12 Choose the correct response.

1 What do you do in the evening?
 a At ten o'clock.
 b I like animals.
 c We watch television.
2 Can I help you?
 a I'd like a pizza, please.
 b Yes, we have.
 c Two pounds fifty.
3 What time do you go to bed?
 a Every morning.
 b At ten o'clock.
 c It's five to nine.
4 Do you usually have a bath or a shower?
 a A bath.
 b At night.
 c Yes, I have.
5 Here you are.
 a Where are you?
 b Yes, please.
 c Thanks.

2 marks per item: .../10 marks

13 Underline the two words in each group with the same sound as *her*.

1 first night hurt
2 both girl work
3 learn mean turn
4 old third world
5 circus purse sport

2 marks per item: .../10 marks

14 Complete the dialogue with the expressions.

Do you like | I do | I don't like | I love | I never play

A: What do you usually do at weekends?
B: Well, (**1**) .... art and I often go to art exhibitions.
A: Who is your favourite artist?
B: I like Van Gogh. (**2**) .... modern art – I don't understand it.
A: (**3**) .... painting?
B: Yes, (**4**) .... I like drawing and painting.
A: Do you do other activities?
B: I like sports but (**5**) .... them. I watch them on TV!

2 marks per item: .../10 marks

15 Complete the email with these words.

and | but | computer | every | support | the | them | too | usually | your

Dear Pascal,
Hi! My name's Luke. I live in London with my family. I've got a brother (**1**) .... a sister. I love football and I play (**2**) .... day after school. My favourite team is Chelsea (**3**) .... I don't go to their matches. I watch (**4**) .... on television. Who do you (**5**) .... ? I love music (**6**) .... I can play (**7**) .... guitar a bit. My favourite band is the Arctic Monkeys. Who's (**8**) .... favourite band? Do you like playing (**9**) .... games? I play with my brother – he (**10**) .... wins!
Best wishes,
Luke

1 mark per item: .../10 marks

Total: .../100

I can...

I can talk about my favourite activities.
I can order food.
I can talk about my daily routine.

PROJECT A restaurant menu

Reading

Read the menu and answer the questions.

Paradise Kitchen

The best restaurant in town!
Open all day, 7 days a week!
Great prices – *main courses from $14!*

Do you like going out to eat with your friends?
Do you enjoy great food?
Do you like food from all over the world?
Do you sometimes only want a snack – not a big meal?
Do you need a place to have a party?
Then Paradise Kitchen is the place for you!

Amazing views – look at the sea while you eat!

24 Cedar Drive, Sydney, NSW, 2261, Australia
Phone (02) 9696 2000 • Fax (02) 9656 3434
Email management@paradise.com.au

Snacks, Salads & Side dishes

Just want a snack? Why not try our popular burgers? We've got vegetarian burgers too, for people who don't eat meat. We've also got lots of sandwiches and a lot of different salads. Try our grilled chicken sandwich with a green salad – delicious and healthy! And they don't cost a lot – look at our prices below!

Original American burgers from	$2.50
Green salad	$3
Tomato salad with cheese	$3.00
Caesar salad with chicken and parmesan cheese	$5
Sandwiches from	$3
Chips or potatoes from	$1.50

Main courses

Main courses from $14
We always use fresh ingredients in all our dishes. We serve everything from traditional dishes to fast food! Can't find what you want on our menu? Then speak to one of our chefs – they can cook anything you want!

We've also got lots of fish dishes and vegetarian dishes, including traditional dishes from North Africa, Syria, Jordan, Israel, Iran and Iraq. We have fresh Lebanese bread every day.

Choose from:

English roast beef
Spanish paella
Italian pasta
Indian curry
Japanese sushi
New York steak
Chicken Kiev

But remember, we are an *international* restaurant – we can cook anything! Why not phone or email us to talk to one of our staff?

Desserts

We have lots of delicious desserts, including healthy fresh fruit for people who are on a diet. Try some of these – *only $8 per person!*

Strawberries and cream
Ice cream
Apple pie

Drinks

Milkshakes	$2.50
Cans	$2
Water	$0.50

Coffee from all over the world!
Tea from India and China

1 When can you eat at the Paradise Kitchen restaurant?
2 Where is the restaurant?
3 What can you see there?
4 What snacks have they got?
5 What can you eat if you don't like meat?
6 How much are the main courses?
7 Can you eat dessert there?
8 What can you drink there?

Project

Write your own menu.

- Choose a good name for your restaurant
- Write some salads and side dishes
- Write some main courses
- Write some desserts and drinks
- Write some typical dishes from your country
- Don't forget to write the prices!
- Find or draw pictures of food for your menu

My home

5

> Grammar

Learn about countable and uncountable nouns, the present continuous, *there is* and *there are* with *a*, *some* and *any*.

> Vocabulary

Learn words for house and furniture, and natural features.

> Skills

Read about 'green' homes, and about homes around the world.

Listen to a radio programme about an eco-house.

Write an email.

> Communicate

Make suggestions, and describe pictures.

1 Describe what you can see in the picture.

2 5.1 Listen. Where are the people?

a in a garden

b in a kitchen

c in a shop

3 What can you see from your bedroom window?

4 What is in your bedroom? Draw a plan. Then work in pairs and tell your partner about it. What have you got in common?

See Vocabulary Explorer: Page 106

5A Home sweet home

Reading and listening

3 5.2 **Read and listen to the dialogue. Where is Brad? Where is his dad, Clark?**

Clark: Hello, Brad! Can you see me?
Brad: No, I can't. The webcam isn't working.
Clark: Just a moment … is it working now?
Brad: Yes, it is. Hi, Dad! Are you working in your study? I can see your books and your cameras.
Clark: Yes, this is our study, our living room, our bedroom and our kitchen all in one room. Look, can you see the microwave? I'm making lunch!
Brad: You're making lunch! But you can't cook! What are you making?
Clark: Microwave pasta! So, Brad, how are you?
Brad: I'm fine. London's fantastic – I love it!
Clark: That's good. And what about school?
Brad: Oh, it's OK. Is Mum there?
Clark: No, she isn't. She's working at the moment. She's with Professor Morris. They're counting penguins.
Brad: Oh! Why?
Clark: Well, the temperature is going up here in the Antarctic and the ice is melting …
Brad: … so the penguins are disappearing.
Clark: That's right. You're a good scientist, Brad!
Brad: Thanks. Hey, Dad, we're doing a project on climate change at school this week. Can you help me with my homework?

Vocabulary

1 **Which of these things can you see in the photos of the Antarctic on page 57?**

cabins cameras doors
ice penguins snow
trees water windows

2 **Which things in Exercise 1 can you count? Which things can't you count? Complete the lists.**

countable nouns: *cabins*
uncountable nouns: *ice*

See Grammar Explorer: Page 124

The Antarctic

8 **Look at a classmate. Write affirmative and negative sentences with these verbs.**

e.g. *Fiona isn't eating.*

eat	look at	play	sit	stand	swim
take	talk	wear	write		

4 **Are the sentences true or false?**

1 The cabin's got four rooms.
2 Brad likes London.
3 Brad's mum is in the cabin.
4 Brad is on holiday this week.

5 **Read the dialogue again and find the words for four rooms of a house. Can you name any other rooms?**

See Vocabulary Explorer: Page 106

Grammar: present continuous (affirmative and negative)

6 **Complete these sentences from the dialogue.**

e.g. I'm *making* lunch.

1 She's .... at the moment.
2 They're .... penguins.
3 The penguins are ....
4 We're .... a project.

7 **Complete the table with short forms.**

Affirmative		
I You/We/They He/She/It	'm (am) (**1**) .... (are) (**2**) .... (is)	studying.
Negative		
I You/We/They He/She/It	'm not (am not) aren't (are not) (**3**) .... (is not)	working.

See Grammar Explorer: Page 124-125

Grammar: present continuous (questions and short answers)

9 **Read the dialogue again. Complete the table.**

Questions		
Am (**1**) .... (**2**)	I you/we/they he/she/it	working?
Short answers		
Yes,	I you/we/they he/she/it	am. are. (**3**) ....
No,	I you/we/they he/she/it	'm not. aren't. (**4**) ....

Grammar Explorer: Page 125

10 **Write questions with the words in Exercise 8.**

e.g. *Is Mandy looking at the teacher?*

11 **Work in pairs. Take turns to mime the activities and guess.**

e.g. **A:** *Are you eating a cake?*
B: *No, I'm not. / Yes, I am.*

Fast finishers

Find the nine letter word. (Clue: Words you can count are ..... .) How many words can you make with the letters?

O	C	B
A	E	U
T	N	L

We're going green.

Vocabulary

1 Look at the poster. Which of these things can you see? What other things can you see?

bags a bath bins a dishwasher a fridge
lights a shower solar panels

See Vocabulary Explorer: Page 106

Reading and listening

2 Read the poster. Complete the poster with words for rooms and parts of a house.

3 5.3 Listen and check your answers.

We're going GREEN in our house! Read about our ECO-HOUSE. You can copy our ideas in your house too.

- In the (**1**) kitchen there is a low-energy fridge. There isn't a dishwasher. Dishwashers use lots of chemicals. There aren't any plastic bags in our ECO-HOUSE – we use strong paper bags.
- In the (**2**) .... there is a separate bin for paper. We only use recycled paper. A tonne of recycled paper can save seventeen trees!
- In the (**3**) .... there is a shower but there isn't a bath. A shower saves water.
- In the (**4**) .... and the (**5**) .... there are low-energy lights to save electricity. And we don't use any aerosols because they are not ecological.
- In the (**6**) .... there are some recycling bins for food, plastic and glass.
- Also there are some solar panels on the (**7**) .... – our ECO-HOUSE can make electricity.

4 **Look at the people in the house. Who is saying each sentence?**

e.g. 'I'm switching off the TV.'
the boy in the living room

1 'We're sending an email birthday card.'
2 'I'm using rechargeable batteries in my camera.'
3 'I'm recycling some bottles.'
4 'I'm switching off the lights.'
5 'I'm saving water.'

Listening

5 5.4 **Listen to a radio programme about the eco-house on the poster. Which things on the poster do the people talk about?**

Grammar: *there is/are* with *a, some, any*

6 **Read the poster again and complete the table.**

Affirmative		
There is There (**2**)	(**1**) .... (**3**)	fridge. solar panels.
Negative		
There isn't There aren't	a (**4**)	dishwasher. plastic bags.

See Grammar Explorer: Page 125

7 **Look at the poster and the things in Exercise 1 again. Write sentences about the things in the house with *there is/ are or there isn't/aren't*.**

e.g. There are some bags in the kitchen.

8 **Study the table.**

Questions		
Is there Are there	a any	bath? solar panels?
Short answers		
Yes, there is. / No, there isn't. Yes, there are. / No, there aren't.		

9 **Write six questions about the eco-house.**

e.g. Are there any solar panels?

Grammar: *some* and *any* with uncountable nouns

10 **Find the names for these uncountable things on the poster.**

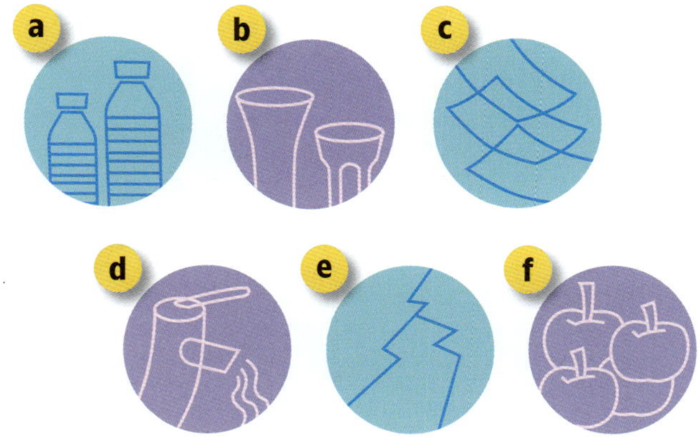

11 **Study the table. Is the verb singular or plural?**

Affirmative		
There's	some	paper.
Negative		
There isn't	any	glass.
Questions		
Is there	any	food?
Short answers		
Yes, there is. / No, there isn't.		

See Grammar Explorer: Page 125

12 **Write affirmative and negative sentences and questions.**

e.g. food in the fridge (**?**)
Is there any food in the fridge?

1 plastic in the bin (✓)
2 snow in the mountains (✗)
3 ice in the Antarctic (**?**)
4 paper in the study (✓)
5 water in this river (✗)

Fast finishers

Find the odd word out in each list. Then write more lists for a partner.

1 camera electricity fridge TV
2 ice river snow water
3 door food house window
4 glass paper plastic tree

5C Making suggestions

Vocabulary

1 **Look at the photo. Which of these things can you see?**

a bed   a chair   a chest of drawers   a cupboard
a rug   shelves   a table   a wardrobe

See Vocabulary Explorer: Page 106

Reading and listening

2 5.5 **Read and listen to the dialogue. What are Anna and Meera doing?**

Meera: Hi! What are you doing?
Anna: I'm moving my furniture out of my bedroom so that we can paint it.
Meera: Cool! What colour are you thinking of?
Anna: I don't know!
Meera: Why don't you paint it pink?
Anna: Hmm, sorry, I don't like pink! I'm not a little girl!
Meera: Hey, I'm joking! OK, what can I do?
Anna: Well, why don't you take my books and CDs from the shelves and put them into the wardrobe?
Meera: OK. That's a good idea.

Meera: What about the bed?
Anna: Let's move it into the hall. Come on, push!
Meera: Uff! Sorry Anna, that's no good! Why don't we push it into the middle of the room?
Anna: Great idea!
Meera: And now we can put the rug and the chair on the bed.
Anna: That's perfect.

Pronunciation: intonation in questions

3 5.6 **Listen and repeat these questions from the dialogue. Notice how the intonation falls.**

1 What are you doing?
2 What colour are you thinking of?
3 What can I do?
4 What about the bed?
5 Why don't we push it into the middle of the room?

4 Find four suggestions Anna and Meera make. What is the response to each suggestion?

5 Make suggestions with *Why don't we/you* and *Let's*.

1 I need a book about monkeys. (**go / library**)
2 I'm hungry. (**make / sandwich**)
3 We're bored. (**watch / DVD**)
4 I love penguins. (**go / zoo**)

USEFUL EXPRESSIONS

Let's go to the park.
Why don't we/you listen to music?
We can make a pizza.
OK. I love making pizzas.
That's a great/good idea.
Sorry, but I don't like going to the park.
I hate listening to music.

Speaking

6 Choose some activities for each day. Use these ideas or invent some of your own.

go to the beach/mountains/park | go to the swimming pool | go for a walk | look at photos | have a party | surf the Internet | watch a DVD | write a text message | play a computer game

a rainy day / your birthday / a summer day

7 Work in pairs. How many suggestions and responses can you make for each day?

e.g. A: *It's a rainy day today. Let's look at photos.*
B: *Sorry, but I don't like looking at photos. Why don't we watch a DVD at my house?*
A: *No, that's boring. Let's make a pizza!*

Pronunciation: the /ɪ/ sound

8 5.7 **Listen to three sentences. Which word do you hear? Remember that the \ɪ\ sound is very short.**

1 **a** it **b** eat
2 **a** this **b** these
3 **a** lives **b** leaves

9 5.8 **Listen to these words. Do they have a short sound or a long sound? Repeat.**

bit | swim | fish | sing | drink | milk | bin | list | chips

10 5.9 **Listen to these sentences. Repeat. Can you get the /ɪ/ sound right?**

1 It's fish and chips for him.
2 The list is in the bin.
3 Drink the milk in this.

Writing: describing a picture

1 Look at the photo. What can you see?

2 Complete the email with the present continuous form of these verbs. Be careful with the spelling!

cook | have | make | play | ~~send~~ | sit | take

Hi Tony,
I (**1**) 'm sending a photo with this email. We (**2**) .... a barbecue in the garden. Sohail (**3**) .... with a football. Claire and Shareen (**4**) .... at the table. Can you see me? I (**5**) .... some meat on the barbecue. Mum is in the kitchen – she (**6**) .... a salad. You can't see dad – he (**7**) .... the photo.
Write to me soon,
Peter

3 Find a photo from a holiday or a day out. Write an email describing the picture.

5D Houses and homes

Reading

1 Work in pairs. Look at the photos and find these things.

a chimney mountains people roofs
shadows snow walls water

2 Read about the photos in an exhibition. Match the descriptions with the photos.

Culture

1 It's evening. Businessmen are preparing to sleep in small 'capsule' hotel rooms. Some men are reading or watching TV. There's a TV, air conditioning and an alarm clock in each capsule.

Place: Japan
Photographer: Paul Chesley

2 It's evening, and the sun is shining on the village. A teenager is cycling to an entrance in the wall. He's coming home at the end of a long day. You can't see any animals or people, but you can imagine his dog is waiting for him.

Place: Syria
Photographer: James Stanfield

3 It's morning. There's a house in the middle of a river. The river is flooded and you can see the tops of trees in the water. A man and his son are in a boat. They're going past the house. The man is looking at a person in the house. You can imagine they are friends or neighbours.

Place: Cambodia
Photographer: Michael S. Yamashita

4 It's morning in this beautiful place. A family home – called a *ger* in the local language – is in front of mountains and a lake. There's a chimney in the centre of the *ger* and you can imagine the people inside are cooking breakfast. There's a motorbike outside and a teenager is running towards it.

Place: Mongolia
Photographer: Gordon Wiltsie

Listening

3 5.10 **Listen to an interview with the exhibition organiser. She is talking about one of the homes. Which photo is it?**

Geography and English

Climate change

Read the climate change fact sheet and answer the questions. Then check your answers in the KEY.

Are you a climate change expert? Spot the false sentence.

1 Climate change is connected to changes in the temperature of the Earth.
2 We can't stop climate change.
3 Cars, factories and aeroplanes affect climate change.
4 The ice caps (the Arctic and the Antarctic) are important in climate change.
5 Climate change affects life for people and for animals.
6 The gas carbon dioxide (CO_2) is important in climate change.

These facts are all true – but only five are the results of climate change. Can you spot the odd one out?

1 The ice in the Arctic and the Antarctic is melting.
2 The weather in many parts of the world is changing.
3 Sea levels are rising.
4 Deserts in Africa and Asia are increasing in size.
5 People are cutting down tropical forests.
6 Some animals and plants are disappearing.

Project

What are you doing to slow down climate change? Think about your home and your school. Make a poster. Look at pages 58 and 59 for ideas.

KEY Sentence 2 is false. Sentence 5 is the odd one out.

TRUE STORY

Kangchenjunga

1 We all know about Mount Everest and K2. But do you know about Kangchenjunga? Read and find out.

We're going to the top!

Like Everest and K2, Kangchenjunga is in the Himalayas. It is 8,586 metres high and it is a very difficult and dangerous mountain to climb. It's cold and windy here – sometimes you can't see the paths. There is snow and ice but there aren't any houses or cabins on the mountain!

Imagine it's May 2009. A team from Spain is climbing to the top of Kangchenjunga. Meet the team ...

Ferran Latorre is making a film about the climb for television. There is snow on the mountains and it is very beautiful. He is the first to reach the top at 2.30 pm!

Edurne Pasaban is the team leader. She gets to the top two hours after Ferran. There are 14 mountains in the world that are over 8,000 metres, and Edurne's ambition is to be the first woman to climb them all. This is number 12! The other members of the team – Asier Izaguirre, Juanito Oiarzabal and Alex Chicon – get to the top with Edurne.

One member of the team, Jorge Egocheaga, does not feel well. He doesn't go to the top. When they are coming down, Alex stays with Edurne. They have problems because of the cold but they get down and they find help. They are all OK!

2 Match the people to the things they say.

1 I'm filming the snow. ....
2 I'm trying to climb all 14 of them. ....
3 I'm not climbing to the top – I'm climbing down because I'm not well. ....
4 The temperature is going down. I am helping Edurne. ....
5 I'm carrying the camera. ....
6 We're waiting for help. ....
7 I'm the first but the others are coming. ....

3 Imagine you are one of the members of the Spanish team. Tell a partner what you are doing. What can you see? How does it feel?

NATIONAL GEOGRAPHIC

6 My school trip

> Grammar

Learn about *going to*, possessive 's' and possessive pronouns

> Vocabulary

Learn words for clothes, and places in a town.

> Skills

Read about fashion, and about UNICEF.

Listen to a clothing analyst explaining what our clothes say about us.

Write a postcard.

> Communicate

Talk about plans, and buy things.

1 Work in pairs. What do you know about the place in the picture?

2 6.1 Listen. What is the conversation about?

a shopping for clothes
b going on holiday
c meeting after school

See Vocabulary Explorer: Page 108

3 Complete the sentences for you. Then work in pairs and tell your partner. What have you got in common?

My favourite place is …
In the holidays, we go to …
My dream holiday is …

6A A school trip

Reading and listening

1 6.2 **Read and listen to the dialogue. What is Anna doing?**

1 Sunday afternoon

Anna: Mum, can you help me pack my suitcase?

Mum: Of course. Are you going to need all these clothes in Paris, Anna?

Anna: Yes, I am! We're going to be there for a week, you know! It's difficult to choose the right clothes.

2 Sunday evening

Meera: Hi, it's me. Are you going to wear your jeans or your black trousers tomorrow?

Anna: My jeans. Black trousers are boring.

Meera: OK, jeans, good idea. See you tomorrow!

3 Monday morning

Anna: Wow, Paris! We're going to have a great time!

Meera: I know, Paris is really exciting! I'm going to climb to the top of the Eiffel Tower …

Anna: … and I'm going to eat croissants …

Meera: … and I'm not going to speak English – only French.

Anna: Well that isn't going to be easy for you!

Meera: What do you mean?

Anna: Your French is terrible!

Mum: Girls, hurry up! You're going to miss the train.

2 Choose the correct answer.

1 Anna and Meera are going to be in Paris for …
a a weekend **b** a week **c** four weeks.

2 Anna is going to wear …
a jeans **b** trousers **c** a T-shirt.

3 Anna thinks speaking French is going to be … for Meera.
a boring **b** difficult **c** easy

Vocabulary

3 Find these adjectives in the dialogue. Are they positive or negative? Find the pairs of opposites.

boring difficult easy exciting great terrible

4 Work in pairs. Tell your partner your opinion of these things. Do you agree or disagree?

computer games English fashion football holidays rap music school trips shopping

e.g. A: *I think football is boring.*
B: *Really? I think it's exciting.*
A: *I think rap music is terrible.*
B: *Me too!*

Grammar: *going to*

5 **Read the dialogue again. What are Anna and Meera's plans for Paris? Complete the sentences.**

1 Meera is going to …
2 Anna is going to …
3 Meera is not going to …

6 **Read the dialogue again and complete the tables.**

Affirmative		
I You/We/They He/She/It	(**1**) .... (am) going to (**2**) .... (are) going to 's (is) going to	visit Paris.
Negative		
I You/We/They He/She/It	(**3**) .... (am not) going to aren't (are not) going to (**4**) .... (is not) going to	miss the train.

Questions		
Am (**5**) .... Is	I you/we/they he/she/it	going to practise French?
Short answers		
Yes, I (**6**) .... Yes, you/we/they are. Yes, he/she/it is.	No, I'm not. No, you/we/they aren't. No, he/she/it isn't.	

See Grammar Explorer: Page 125

7 **Write sentences with *going to*.**

e.g. they / take / photos of Paris
They're going to take photos of Paris.

1 we / see / the Louvre Museum
2 Anna / buy / souvenirs
3 I / speak / English
4 he / wear / jeans
5 you / telephone / your mum every day
6 they / practise / French
7 he / stay / with his pen pal
8 we / eat / French food

8 **Work in pairs. Look at the pictures. How many answers can you write for each question?**

e.g. *1 Because he's going to make a sandwich.*

1 Why is he in the kitchen?

2 Why is she leaving the house?

3 Why is she turning on the computer?

4 Why is he at the shops?

9 **Write questions with *you* + *going to* and these words. Match the questions (1–6) with the answers (a–f). Then listen and check.**

e.g. *1 Where are you going to go? f*

1 Where / go?
2 Who / go with?
3 What / do there?
4 What clothes / take?
5 Where / eat?
6 When / go there?

a In July.
b In a restaurant.
c My cousins.
d Shorts and a T-shirt.
e Visit the Eiffel Tower.
f To Paris.

10 **Work in pairs. Choose one of these places and plan five things to do there. Then work with a different partner. Talk about your plans.**

the beach **a big city** **a sports complex**

e.g. A: *Where are you going to go?*
B: *To the beach.*
A: *What are you going to do there?*
B: *I'm going to swim in the sea.*

Fast finishers

Think of a place for each letter of the alphabet.

Australia, Beijing, city, D…

6B Fashion and you

What do your clothes say about you?

People's clothes say a lot about them. Read about four teenagers' different styles.

1 James's hero is Rafael Nadal – and you can see that in James's clothes. His T-shirt is typical of Nadal's style. In fact, James always buys clothes just like Rafael's if he can.

2 Charlie's favourite music is rap and fashion is a big part of this music. Charlie usually wears baggy jeans and big T-shirts – or jackets with hoods. His dad often travels to the USA and he buys clothes for Charlie there. Where do you buy yours?

3 Fiona's hair is very long and her skirts are always long too. She sometimes wears trousers, but she prefers dresses or skirts. Fiona's style is a version of the 1960s fashions. In fact, the top she is wearing isn't hers – it's her grandmother's. The top is fifty years old!

4 Lynne's style isn't popular with a lot of adults, but her parents' advice is 'Be yourself!' All of Lynne's clothes are black – her boots, her dress and her jacket too. Lynne dyes her hair black. She also wears black eye make-up – but not for school.

Vocabulary

1 **Match these styles with the photos (a–d). Which style do you prefer?**

goth hip hop hippy sporty

2 **Look at the photos. Which clothes have you got? Work in pairs and tell your partner.**

e.g. *I've got some trainers but I haven't got any black boots.*

See Vocabulary Explorer: Page 108

Reading and listening

3 6.3 **Read and listen to the texts. Match the texts (1–4) with the photos (a–d).**

4 **Read the texts again. Are the sentences true or false? Correct the false sentences.**

e.g. James's style is hip hop.
F James's style is sports.

1 James likes Nadal's style.
2 Charlie's dad is American.
3 Fiona's grandmother is fifty years old.
4 Lynne's hair isn't naturally black.

Grammar: possessive 's'

5 **Complete these sentences from the article.**

1 .... clothes say a lot about them.
2 .... hero is Rafael Nadal.
3 Her .... advice is 'Be yourself!'
4 All of .... clothes are black.

6 **Study the position of the apostrophe in the examples (a–d). Then match the sentences in Exercise 5 with the examples.**

The possessive form of nouns		
a Singular noun/name	Lynne's	clothes
b Singular noun/name ending in *s*	James's	
c Plural noun	teenagers'	
d Irregular plural noun	people's	

See Grammar Explorer: Page 126

7 **Put the apostrophe (') in the correct place.**

e.g. Both the models shoes are pretty.
Both the models' shoes are pretty.

1 Charlies T-shirt is blue.
2 Jamess trainers are old.
3 All the teenagers clothes are fashionable.
4 The long skirt is Fionas.
5 Both boys hair is short.
6 Lynne isn't wearing childrens clothes.

8 **Write six sentences – some true and some false – about the photos. Then work in pairs and exchange your sentences. Correct your partner's false sentences.**

e.g. Charlie's jacket is yellow and blue.

Grammar: possessive pronouns

9 **Complete the table with the possessive pronouns.**

hers his ~~mine~~ ours theirs yours

Subject pronouns	Possessive pronouns
I	(1) mine
you	(2) ....
he	(3) ....
she	(4) ....
we	(5) ....
they	(6) ....

See Grammar Explorer: Page 126

10 **Write possessive pronouns.**

e.g. This isn't my sweatshirt. Mine is big.

1 The gloves are Lynne's. They're ....
2 The sunglasses are Charlie's. They're ....
3 Excuse me. That's my jacket. It's ....
4 The blue car is my parents' car. It's ....
5 Suzy, this isn't my bag. Is it .... ?
6 Our names are on the tickets. They're ....

Fast finishers

Find the odd word out in each list. Then write more lists for a partner.

1 exciting great terrible nice
2 boots gloves sandals shoes
3 cap hippy scarf skirt
4 goth hip hop reggae sporty

6C Shopping

Vocabulary

1 Match the symbols with the money and the countries.

	1	= 100	
£	euro	pence	Ireland, France, Spain, etc.
€	dollar	cents	the UK
$	pound	cents	the USA

2 6.4 **Listen and repeat**

20p 95p £1.00 £2.50 £5.99 £20

Reading and listening

3 6.5 **Anna is going to buy presents for her pen pal's family in France. Look at the pictures and listen. What does Anna buy? What can't she buy?**

Anna: Excuse me.
Assistant: Yes, can I help you?
Anna: How much are the key rings, please?
Assistant: They're (**1**) .... each.
Anna: OK. I'd like these two key rings, please. And how much is this cap?
Assistant: It's (**2**) ....
Anna: Hmm. Meera, do you like this cap?
Meera: Yes, I think it's great.
Anna: OK. I'd like this cap too, please. Good, now I've got my presents.
Assistant: Anything else?
Anna: Yes, can I have these postcards, too? And have you got any stamps?
Assistant: I'm sorry, we haven't got any stamps at the moment. But there's a post office in this street.
Anna: OK, thanks.
Assistant: So, four postcards at (**3**) .... each, two key rings and the cap. That's (**4**) ...., please.
Anna: Here you are.
Assistant: And here's your change, (**5**) ....
Anna: Thank you very much.

See Vocabulary Explorer: Page 109

4 6.5 **Read and listen to the dialogue again. Complete the dialogue with these prices.**

30p 83p £1.49 £4.99 £9.17

Pronunciation: sentence stress

5 6.6 **Listen and repeat these questions from the dialogue. Which words are stressed? Which words are unstressed?**

1 How much are the key rings?
2 How much is this cap?

6 **Invent prices for the things in the pictures. Work in pairs. Ask and answer questions.**

e.g. A: *How much are the calendars?*
B: *They're £5.99 each.*
A: *How much is this fridge magnet?*
B: *It's £1.50.*

7 **Look at the *Useful expressions*. Write C for customer or A for assistant next to each expression.**

USEFUL EXPRESSIONS

Anything else?
Can I help you?
Excuse me.
Have you got any stamps?
Here you are.
How much are the mugs?
How much is this T-shirt?
I'd like three fridge magnets.
That's four ninety-nine please.

Speaking

8 **Work in pairs. You are in the shop in the photo. Take turns to be the customer and the assistant. You've got £10. Buy presents for your family or friends.**

Pronunciation: unstressed sound /ə/

9 6.7 **Listen. Notice that the underlined part of these words is stressed. What sound can you hear in the unstressed part? Repeat.**

album	breakfast	desert	London
August	children	famous	ocean
autumn	chocolate	fashion	parents
Belgium	circus	island	sentence

10 6.8 **Listen and practise these sentences.**

1 Do children in Belgium have chocolate for breakfast?
2 London is famous for fashion shows.
3 He's on a desert island in the Indian Ocean.

Writing: a postcard

1 **Read the postcard from Anna's pen pal. Complete the postcard with the *going to* form of these verbs.**

buy come go have see write

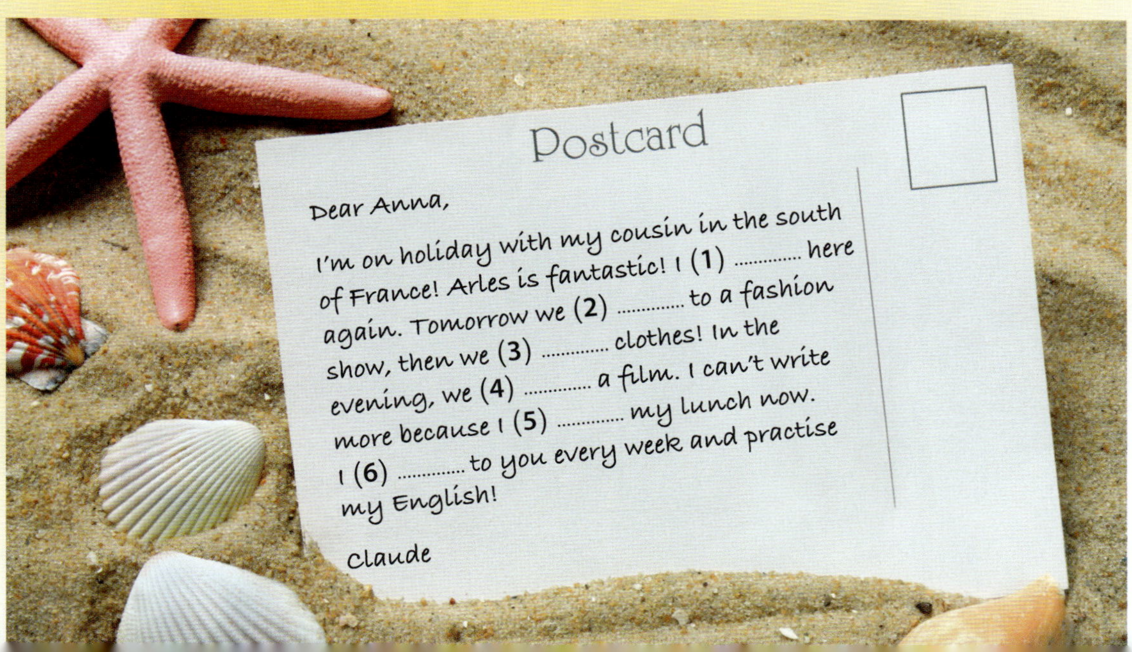

Postcard

Dear Anna,

I'm on holiday with my cousin in the south of France! Arles is fantastic! I (1) .... here again. Tomorrow we (2) .... to a fashion show, then we (3) .... clothes! In the evening, we (4) .... a film. I can't write more because I (5) .... my lunch now. I (6) .... to you every week and practise my English!

Claude

2 **Write a postcard to a friend. Imagine you are at one of the places in Exercise 10 on page 67. Write about the place and your plans.**

6D UNICEF and schools

Culture

Reading

1 **Ewan McGregor has two jobs. What you think they are? Read the first part of the article and check your answer.**

2 6.9 **Read 'Day for Change' and complete the article with these questions. Then listen and check your answers.**

a Where does the money go?
b What is UNICEF Day for Change?
c What do you do in this activity?

2003 Ewan McGregor, star of *Moulin Rouge*, *Star Wars* and *Angels and Demons*, plans a trip around the world on his motorbike.

2004 On Ewan's trip, he visits schools in Ukraine, Kazakhstan and Mongolia.

2005 Ewan decides he's going to help children around the world. He becomes a UNICEF Ambassador.

NOW Ewan visits UNICEF projects around the world and he helps to raise money for UNICEF.

Ewan McGregor, UNICEF Ambassador

Day for Change

1 .... Leave your school uniform at home for a day and raise money for schools around the world.

£3.80 buys a desk.

2 .... You wear your favourite clothes to school for one day and you give some money to UNICEF. You can wear fancy dress or your ordinary clothes – you can choose. Talk to your teacher to organise Day for Change at your school. Visit www. unicef.org.uk/dayforchange.

12p buys a bar of soap.

3 .... Your money helps children and schools in different countries. There are lots of schools around the world without books, desks or water.

£1 buys a 20-litre water container.

Listening

3 6.10 **Listen to Peter. He's talking about Day for Change at his school. Choose the correct answers.**

1. Peter's school's day for change is **1st March / 1st May**.
2. He's going to wear **ordinary clothes / fancy dress**.
3. They're going to wear clothes from ***Star Wars / The Golden Compass***.
4. The money is going to **Romania / Ukraine**.
5. Ewan McGregor is **Peter's / Peter's friend's** favourite actor.

4 **What is this school going to do with the money from Day for Change? Choose the correct caption.**

1. Aja's school in Gambia is going to use the Day for Change money to plant a school garden.
2. Nelson's school in Kenya is going to buy more laboratory equipment.
3. Samir's school in India is going to spend Day for Change money on new desks and chairs.

Social Science and English

NGOs

1 **Read about NGOs and choose the correct answers to the questions.**

1. What do NGOs do?
   - **a** They work with communities.
   - **b** They help governments.
   - **c** They work for UNICEF.
2. Where do they work?
   - **a** They work in the UK.
   - **b** They are international, national and local.
   - **c** They are international organisations.
3. How can you help NGOs?
   - **a** You can go to London.
   - **b** You can volunteer and raise money.
   - **c** You can answer their problems.

NGO is short for Non-Government Organisation. UNICEF is an example of an NGO. NGOs help people in many ways. For example, communities sometimes have problems with health or education. Or they have problems after a natural disaster – tsunamis, volcanoes or hurricanes. NGOs work with these communities. They help them find answers to the problems. NGOs can be international (for example, UNICEF), national (Barnardo's is a British NGO which helps children and young people) and local (Thames Reach works with homeless people in London). You can take part in the work of NGOs – you can raise money or be a volunteer.

Question:

What have these famous names got in common?

Angelina Jolie · **Bill Gates** · **Bob Geldof**

Bono · **Claudia Schiffer** · **Elle Macpherson** · **Liv Tyler**

Lucy Liu · **Robbie Williams** · **Sting**

Answer: They all help the work of NGOs.

2 **Work in pairs. Tell your partner about an NGO activity you know about – a rock concert or a sports event, for example.**

Project

Find out who are UNICEF ambassadors in your country. Go to the UNICEF website and read about activities your school can do.

Review Units 5 and 6

Vocabulary

1 Write the names of the rooms where you …

1 sleep ....
2 watch TV ....
3 have a shower ....
4 make lunch ....
5 do your homework ....

1 mark per item: …/5 marks

2 Name the items of furniture.

1 ....
2 ....
3 ....
4 ....
5 ....

1 mark per item: …/5 marks

3 Write the opposites.

1 good b..............
2 boring e..............
3 easy d..............
4 terrible g..............
5 happy s..............

1 mark per item: …/5 marks

4 Complete the sentences with the correct words.

caps coats gloves shorts skirts jackets sunglasses trainers

1 We can't wear .... for school – only brown or black shoes.
2 Boys don't usually wear ....
3 Tennis players often wear white .... and a white T-shirt.
4 Protect your eyes with ....
5 I love American baseball ....

1 mark per item: …/5 marks

5 Name the things.

1 ....
2 ....
3 ....
4 ....
5 ....

1 mark per item: …/5 marks

Grammar

1 Look at the pictures. Write sentences with the present continuous form of the verbs.

1 .... (eat)
2 .... (read)
3 .... (not sleep)
4 .... (not / walk)
5 .... (sit)

1 mark per item: …/5 marks

7 Complete the sentences with *a* or *some*.

1 There's .... window in the cabin.
2 Our house has got .... solar panels.
3 There's .... book on the table.
4 There's .... snow in the garden.
5 She's got .... dishwasher.

1 mark per item: …/5 marks

8 Write affirmative (✓) or negative (✗) sentences and questions (?) with the words and *there is / there are*.

1 food in the fridge (?) ....
2 electricity in the house (✗) ....
3 snow in the mountains (✓) ....
4 plastic in the bin (✓) ....
5 water in the river (?) ....

1 mark per item: …/5 marks

9 Complete the sentences with *going to*.

1 .... a pie. (I / not buy)
2 .... a shower? (you / have)
3 .... this DVD. (we / watch)
4 .... lunch? (he / make)
5 .... English. (she / not speak)

1 mark per item: …/5 marks

10 Complete the sentences.

1 This is Anna's bag. It's ....
2 Are .... any penguins in the Arctic?
3 Peter, is this jacket .... or is it Mark's?
4 This is our car. It's ....
5 There aren't .... bins in our street.

1 mark per item: …/5 marks

Communicate

11 Complete the dialogue with the expressions.

Let's | I love | Sorry, but | That's a great idea. | Why don't

Mark: Look at the snow! What can we do?
Jill: (**1**) .... go skiing.
Mark: (**2**) .... I haven't got any skis.
Jill: OK. (**3**) .... we have a snowball fight?
Mark: (**4**) .... You and Ross can fight. I can watch you.
Jill: OK. (**5**) .... making snowballs!

2 marks per item: .../10 marks

12 Match the statements with the responses.

1 Excuse me.
2 How much are the T-shirts?
3 Have you got any caps?
4 Anything else?
5 That's four ninety-nine, please.

a No, thank you.
b Yes, can I help you?
c I'm sorry, we don't sell them.
d They're £8.99 each.
e Here you are.

2 marks per item: .../10 marks

13 Choose the correct response.

1 I'm bored.
  a What can I do?
  b That's a good idea.
  c Why don't you read a book?
2 I'd like this cap, please.
  a Here's your change.
  b That's four euros, please.
  c No, thanks.
3 Why are you going to visit Paris?
  a I learn French.
  b I'm going to learn French.
  c I'm not learning French.
4 Let's go swimming tomorrow.
  a No, I'm sorry.
  b Sorry, I don't like swimming.
  c Yes, I do.
5 Look at him. What's he doing?
  a He's writing an email.
  b He's going to meet his pen pal next week.
  c He plays a computer game.

2 marks per item: .../10 marks

14 Write the present continuous verbs with the correct spelling.

1 We're .... lunch in a restaurant. (**have**)
2 I'm not .... a coat today. (**wear**)
3 We're .... a project on climate change. (**do**)
4 Dad's .... some photos. (**take**)
5 The dog's .... under the table. (**sit**)
6 My brother's .... at home. (**study**)
7 My sister's .... with her toys. (**play**)
8 What are you ....? (**eat**)
9 That dog's ....! (**swim**)
10 Is he .... the microwave? (**use**)

1 mark per item: .../10 marks

15 Complete the email with the correct form of the verbs.

Hi Jill,

I (**1**) .... (**write**) this email at the airport. We (**2**) .... (**wait**) for the plane. We (**3**) .... (**go**) on holiday to Spain. My pen pal's family (**4**) .... (**meet**) us at the airport. We've got lots of plans. We (**5**) .... (**see**) a flamenco dance, and my mum (**6**) .... (**lie**) on the beach every day! But I (**7**) .... (**not / watch**) a bullfight. I think they're horrible. I (**8**) .... (**go**) shopping! Oh, time to go – they (**9**) .... (**call**) our plane. I can see my mum – she (**10**) .... (**look for**) me!

See you soon,

Kelly

mark per item: .../10 marks

Total: .../100

I can...

I can make suggestions.
I can describe pictures.
I can talk about things.
I can buy things.

PROJECT Welcome to my home!

Reading

Read the article and answer the questions.

Hi! Welcome to my home! My name is Javier. I live in Guadalajara in Mexico.

I can speak Spanish and English, but we only speak Spanish at home because my parents can't speak English. I live with my mum, dad, and my sister, Martha.

We live in a big flat on the third floor. I like it very much because it's very clean and comfortable. The walls are painted bright colours and I like that too. It has got air conditioning in each room.

There are three bedrooms in the flat. In my room, there are two beds because sometimes my cousin, Hector, comes to stay. I haven't got a wardrobe but my sister has – she's got a lot of clothes! There's a desk in my room too. That's where I like doing my homework. I like listening to music in my room too.

My favourite room in the house is the living room. I like watching TV and DVDs in there. Sometimes I play video games in there with my friends or with my cousin.

Sometimes Mum cooks in the kitchen and we sometimes eat on the balcony. I enjoy sitting outside with my family and friends. It's very relaxing. Sometimes we have parties out there, and that's always a lot of fun!

1 Where does Javier live?
2 Who does he live with?
3 Can his parents speak English?
4 Which floor is the flat on?
5 Has his flat got air conditioning?
6 Why are there two beds in Javier's room?
7 Where does he like doing his homework?
8 Which is his favourite room? Why?
9 Where do they sometimes eat?
10 Where do they have parties?

Project

Make a poster and write about your own home.

- Draw a plan of your home
- Write the names of the rooms
- Put pictures of people or furniture in the rooms
- Write about the rooms
- Don't forget to say what you like doing in the rooms

NATIONAL GEOGRAPHIC

My history

7

> Grammar

Learn about the past simple of *be*, the past simple of regular and irregular verbs.

> Vocabulary

Learn adjectives and past tense adverbs.

> Skills

Read about family histories, and about festivals with fire.

Listen to a biography.

Write an invitation and a reply.

> Communicate

Talk about past activities, and make, accept or decline invitations.

1 **Work in pairs. What does the picture make you think about?**

2 7.1 **Listen to an interview and complete the information.**

Age: (**1**) ....

Things he remembers: (**2**) .... (**3**) .... (**4**) ....

3 **Answer the questions for yourself. Then ask your partner.**

1 What is your first memory?

2 What can you remember about your first …

• birthday party • day at school? • holiday?

3 What are your favourite family occasions? Why?

See Vocabulary Explorer: Page 110

7A Celebrations

Reading and listening

1 7.2 **Match the photos (a–c) with the occasions. Then read, listen and check.**

a birthday party   a christening
a Mother's Day celebration   a New Year's Eve party
a summer holiday   a wedding

1

Mum: Look, this is our wedding photo.
Brad: Wow! Look at your clothes!
Mum: It was twenty years ago. Those clothes were very fashionable!
Brad: Were they? Are you sure? Wow!
Mum: Anna, look at your dad's face!
Anna: Was he nervous?
Mum: I think he was scared of my father – Granddad Mark!

2

Mum: Here's Anna at her christening. Look at her happy face!
Anna: How old was I in this photo?
Mum: You were about six months old.
Brad: You were a fat baby!
Mum: Yes, she was always hungry.
Anna: Excuse me! I was very small when I was born.

3

Anna: Oh, I remember this holiday. It was in Spain, in 2004. It was a great holiday!
Mum: It was very hot – the sand and the sea were really hot!
Brad: Were you ill, Anna? Or tired? You look terrible.
Mum: I think she was ill from the boat trip.
Anna: Mum! Brad! I wasn't ill or tired, and it wasn't hot. It was a fantastic holiday!

2 **Are the sentences true or false?**

1 Anna's dad was nervous at the wedding.
2 Anna was two months old at her christening.
3 Anna was a fat baby.
4 Anna and her family were on holiday in Spain.

Vocabulary

3 **Which adjectives are not in the dialogue? Check the meanings in your dictionary.**

bored **excited** **happy** **hungry** **ill** **nervous** **scared** **tired**

See Vocabulary Explorer: Page 110

Grammar: past simple *be*

4 **Complete the sentences from the dialogue.**

1 Those clothes .... very fashionable!
2 He .... scared.
3 You .... a fat baby!
4 It .... in Spain.

5 **Complete the tables.**

Affirmative		
I/He/She/It You/We/They	(1) .... (2)	happy.
Negative		
I/He/She/It You/We/They	(3) .... weren't	hungry.

Questions		
Was (4)	I/he/she/it you/we/they	in Spain?
Short answers		
Yes,	I/he/she/it you/we/they	(5) .... were.
No,	I/he/she/it you/we/they	(6) .... weren't.

See Grammar Explorer: Page 126

6 **Complete the sentences with *was* or *were*.**

e.g. The wedding ..was.. in 2008.

1 Our parents .... happy.
2 The bride's wedding dress .... beautiful.
3 The party .... in a hotel.
4 We .... excited.
5 You .... in every photo.
6 It .... a great day.

7 **Write questions about a wedding party. Then write answers.**

e.g. bride / nervous (✗)
Was the bride nervous? No, she wasn't.

1 food / delicious (✓)
2 guests / happy (✓)
3 weather / bad (✗)
4 flowers / beautiful (✓)
5 music / good (✓)

8 **Put the words in order and write questions.**

1 were / when / born / you?
2 born / were / where / you?
3 first pet / what / your / was?
4 best friend / your / who / at primary school / was?
5 first teacher / was / your / who?

9 **Work in pairs. Ask and answer the questions in Exercise 8.**

10 **Complete the time expressions with these words.**

2008 **days** **evening** **half past ten** **year**

e.g. at eight o'clock / half past ten / midday

1 yesterday morning / afternoon / ....
2 last night / week / month / .... / Saturday
3 two hours / .... / weeks / years ago
4 in 2006 / ....

11 **Prepare five questions for your partner using *where* and the expressions in Exercise 10. Then work in pairs. Ask and answer questions.**

e.g. **A:** *Where were you last Saturday?*
B: *I was at a football match.*

Fast finishers

Write the words. Which letter is in all the words?

1 Four weeks is a _ _ _ _ _ .
2 A picture from a camera is a _ _ _ _ _ .
3 Things you wear are _ _ _ _ _ _ _ .
4 The opposite of cold is _ _ _ .

7B Strange coincidences

Their 32nd birthday – their first party together

Last year, Jerry Levey and Mark Newman celebrated a very special birthday. Jerry and Mark are twin brothers, but it was their first birthday party together. When they were babies, two different families adopted them. They lived in different towns and their lives were completely separate. When they became adults, Jerry and Mark both worked as drivers and then they both started jobs in the fire service. Then, when they were thirty-two, Jerry finally discovered his brother Mark. The two brothers looked exactly the same. Jerry says, 'All my life, there was something missing. Now, I'm happy.'

Special connections?

Jenny and Angela Frost were born on the same day fourteen years ago. They are identical twins. When they were babies, it was impossible to see the difference between them. Sometimes, the twins' mum was confused! When they began to talk, they had a special language. When they were nine, they both had toothache in the same tooth at the same time. The twins' friends said, 'At parties, we never played guessing games with Jenny and Angela. They always won because they read each other's minds!'

Reading and listening

1 7.3 **Read and listen to the texts again and choose the correct answers.**

1 Jenny and Angela are … now.
 a one year old b nine years old
 c fourteen years old

2 They had a special language when they were …
 a babies. b at school. c at parties.

3 At the age of nine, they had …
 a a game. b toothache. c lots of friends.

4 Jerry and Mark lived with …
 a their parents. b the same family.
 c different families.

5 They worked in …
 a the same town. b the same jobs.
 c different jobs.

6 They were reunited …
 a last year. b last month. c last week.

Grammar: past simple regular verbs (affirmative)

2 **Find these verbs in the article about Jerry and Mark. Find three more verbs with the same ending.**

celebrated adopted lived worked

3 **Study the table.**

Regular verbs affirmative		
I/You/He/She/It/ We/You/They	lived worked	in different towns.

The past simple has only one form. We add *-ed* or only *-d* when the verb ends in *-e*.

See Grammar Explorer: Page 127

4 **Complete the sentences with the past simple form of these verbs.**

arrive celebrate cook invite
look open play

e.g. My sister *celebrated* her birthday with a party.

1 We .... our friends and family.
2 They .... at eight o'clock.
3 Tina .... 'Happy Birthday' on the piano.
4 You .... a bottle of champagne.
5 My dad .... some delicious food.
6 My sister .... very happy.

Listening

5 7.4 **The words below are in a biography of some famous twins. Which twins do you think the biography is about? Listen and check your answer.**

changed divorced formed played
recorded started travelled

Bob and Mike Bryan – tennis players

Mary-Kate and Ashley Olsen – actresses

Tom and Bill Kaulitz – singers in the band Tokio Hotel

6 **Match the notes with one of the other two photos. Then write sentences about the twins using the notes.**

start / playing tennis / two years old
enter / first competition aged six
always / practise together
never / play against each other
study / Stanford University 1996-8
join / professional tennis circuit 1995

Grammar: past simple irregular verbs (affirmative)

7 **Find the past simple form of these verbs in the article about Jenny and Angela.**

begin have read say win

The pronunciation of the past simple form *read* is /red/.

See Vocabulary Explorer: Page 111

8 **Complete the table with the past simple form of the verbs.**

took bought drank saw went came
ate wrote gave made

Irregular verbs

Infinitive	Past simple	Infinitive	Past simple
buy	(**1**)	go	(**6**) ....
come	(**2**)	make	(**7**) ....
drink	(**3**)	see	(**8**) ....
eat	(**4**)	take	(**9**) ....
give	(**5**)	write	(**10**) ....

9 7.5 **Complete the story with the past simple form of the verbs. Then listen and check.**

When I (**1**) *was* (**be**) ten, I (**2**) .... (**have**) a fantastic Christmas. Our family (**3**) .... (**come**) to our house for lunch. My mum (**4**) .... (**make**) an enormous meal and my parents (**5**) .... (**drink**) champagne. Then we (**6**) .... (**give**) each other presents. My dad (**7**) .... (**buy**) me a camera. I (**8**) .... (**take**) photos of the family and the tree. The dog (**9**) .... (**eat**) the paper from the presents!

10 **Think about five interesting moments in your life. Write five sentences – four true and one false. Then work in pairs and exchange your sentences. Find your partner's false sentence.**

e.g. *When I was six, I ate a spider.*

Fast finishers

Match the verbs with opposite meanings. How many other pairs of verbs do you know?

close finish give lose open
play start take win work

7C Invitations

Reading and listening

1 7.6 **Read and listen to the dialogue. What's the celebration?**

Brad: Hi, can I speak to Harry, please?
Harry's mum: Yes, who is it, please?
Brad: It's Brad.
Harry's mum: Oh - hello, Brad. Just a moment.
Harry: Hi, Brad. What's up?
Brad: Well, you remember that my parents arrived from Antarctica last week?
Harry: Yes, of course.
Brad: We're going to have a big party for them next weekend. Would you like to come?
Harry: Thanks, I'd love to!
Brad: Great. Meera and your parents can come too, of course.
Harry: OK. Where's the party?
Brad: It's at Anna's house. It's on Saturday at seven o'clock.
Harry: OK, see you on Saturday!
Brad: Oh, Harry, it's a fancy dress party. The theme is … the South Pole!

2 Answer the questions.

1 Is the party for Brad or for his parents?
2 Is Harry going to go to the party?
3 Where is the party?
4 When is it?

3 What does Brad say to invite Harry? What is Harry's response?

4 Match the cards (1–3) with the invitations (a–c).

1

a *Beth and Ryan would like you to join them to celebrate their marriage at The Bridge Hotel, Corbridge.*

2

b **Party! Party!**
I'm 18 on the 18th! Come to my party and bring lots of friends.

3

c *Toby Burton's christening is on June 17th.*

USEFUL EXPRESSIONS

Would you like to come to our party?
Do you want to play tennis on Friday?
Please come / play / go with us.
Thanks, I'd love to.
I'm sorry, I can't.
on Friday
at 7 o'clock / our house

Speaking

5 Work in pairs. Take turns to invite your partner to do these things.

go on holiday | go shopping | go to the cinema
have a burger | play football | play a video game

e.g. A: *Do you want to play football?*
B: *Yes, I'd love to. Where?*
A: *At school.*
B: *When?*
A: *On Friday.*
B: *What time?*
A: *At eight o'clock.*

Pronunciation: *-ed* endings

6 7.7 **Listen to the endings of the verbs. Repeat.**

1 /t/ looked
2 /d/ stayed
3 /ɪd/ started

7 7.8 **Listen to these verbs and write them in the table. Repeat.**

~~arrived~~ ~~celebrated~~ climbed ~~cooked~~ helped invited lived opened packed telephoned travelled worked

1 /t/	2 /d/	3 /ɪd/
cooked	arrived	celebrated

8 7.9 **Listen and repeat. Be careful with the *-ed* sound and how the words link together.**

1 We arrived in Edinburgh.
2 They cooked us a meal.
3 The party started at eight o'clock.

Writing: an invitation and a reply

1 Complete the sentences with the correct preposition.

at at in on on

1 She was born .... Tuesday.
2 The wedding is .... April.
3 The party is .... eight o'clock.
4 We live .... 23 London Road.
5 My birthday is .... February 28th.

2 Read the sentences. Are they from an invitation (I) or a reply (R)?

a We hope you can come. ......I......
b It's at Zoe's house at 8 p.m. on Friday.
c I'd love to come to your party.
d Please come to our party and celebrate with us!
e Congratulations on your exam results!

3 Complete the invitation and the reply with the sentences (a–e) in Exercise 2 in the correct order.

4 Write an invitation to a special occasion. Then work in pairs. Exchange invitations with your partner and write a reply.

7D Festivals with fire

Reading

1 Look at the photos of four celebrations in the UK. What can you see? Match these words with the photos.

a fire | fireworks | a guy | a party | stones | the sunrise | torches

Bonfire Night

Up Helly Aa

Hogmanay

Culture

Bonfire Night

On 5th November 1605, a group of men tried to kill King James I in the Houses of Parliament in London. One of the men, Guy Fawkes, made a 'bomb' to start a fire. But the plan failed and the King's men arrested Guy Fawkes. Now, on Bonfire Night, people in the UK make a 'guy' and burn it on a bonfire.

Up Helly Aa

The Up Helly Aa festival is in the Shetland Islands north of Scotland. It began in about 1870 and it celebrates the Vikings. At the end of January, in towns on the islands, people wear Viking clothes and carry torches in the streets. Then they burn a Viking boat and have a great party all night.

Hogmanay

Hogmanay is the New Year's Eve celebration in Scotland and the north of England. On 31st December, there is an enormous party in Edinburgh with fireworks, singing and dancing. Everyone sings a special song about friends and family. Its name is Auld Lang Syne.

Summer Solstice

People go to Stonehenge, in the south of England, to celebrate the middle of summer. At the Summer Solstice celebration, people light fires and torches, and they watch the sky all night. Then in the morning they watch the sunrise between the stones of Stonehenge.

Summer Solstice

2 **Read the text. Are the sentences true or false?**

1 People celebrate Bonfire Night in summer.
2 Guy Fawkes wanted to kill the King.
3 The King burned in a fire.
4 Guy Fawkes arrested the King's men.

Chemistry and English

Fire

1 **Read about fire and answer the questions.**

1 How did people use fire?
2 Why is oxygen important in fire?

2 **Work in pairs. Think of two ways we use fire in everyday life. Compare your ideas with the class.**

Fires happen naturally. Every summer there are forest fires in many countries. These fires can be dangerous and they can also be useful. A long time ago, people learned to control natural fires. Fire was extremely important in human history. It gave people light and heat. People used fire to see at night and to stay warm in winter. They also used it to cook food and to make metal tools.

Fire is a chemical reaction. Oxygen and other materials burn together. You can't have fire without oxygen. The reaction makes energy. This energy is the light and the heat that we use. For example, oxygen and petrol burn in your car engine. When oxygen and petrol burn, the reaction makes water (H_2O) and carbon dioxide (CO_2), and it also makes the energy that drives your car.

3 **Read about the celebrations again and complete the table.**

	bonfire night	Up Helly Aa	Summer solstice	Hogmanay
Where is it?		*the Shetland Islands*		
When is it?			*the middle of summer*	
What does it celebrate?	*the king was safe*			
What do people do?				*there are fireworks, singing and dancing*

Listening

4 7.10 **Listen to Adam talking about his favourite festival. Which festival is it?**

Project

Work in pairs and make a festival poster. Find a photo of a festival in your country. Find the answers to the questions in Exercise 3 and write a paragraph about the festival.

TRUE STORY

A modern-day explorer

1 What do you think about when you imagine an explorer? Discuss the following questions with a partner before you read the article:

Do you think of someone who is old or young?

What kind of life does he/she have?

David de Rothschild

David de Rothschild was born in London in 1978. When he finished his studies in Oxford and London, he started an organisation called Adventure Ecology. He wanted to find a way to show people that we can help the planet. But David didn't want an easy or a boring job – he's a modern-day explorer and he believes that saving the Earth is an adventure!

In 2005, David travelled across Antarctica and went to the South Pole. A year later, he travelled from Russia to Canada across the Arctic. This time, he went to the North Pole and a hungry polar bear wanted to eat him! Then, in 2007, he went to Ecuador in South America.

David is also the man who started the Plastiki project – an expedition to cross the Pacific Ocean in a boat made from plastic bottles. David knew there were a lot of problems – like pollution of the sea and rising sea levels. He wanted to make people excited about finding answers to these problems.

2 Answer these questions about David de Rothschild:

1. When was he born?
2. Where was he a student?
3. What is the name of the organisation that he started?
4. Is his job boring or interesting?
5. Where was he in 2005?
6. What happened to him at the North Pole?
7. What was the Plastiki project?

3 Read *How to be a good adventurer* and discuss these questions with a partner:

1. Do you think you would make a good explorer? Why? / Why not?
2. Where would you like to explore (forests, the jungle, the oceans, space, Antarctica, etc)? Say why.

How to be a good adventurer

1. Enjoy yourself!
2. Be prepared for anything – always plan ahead.
3. Always do what your heart tells you to do.
4. Take lots of photos and write things down.
5. Have people in your team you can trust.

NATIONAL GEOGRAPHIC

My stories

8

> Grammar

Learn about past simple questions and short answers, negative forms and adverbs of manner.

> Vocabulary

Learn words for technology, and learn adverbs and irregular verbs.

> Skills

Read about famous inventions, and about astronomers.

Listen to information from a museum.

Write a story.

> Communicate

Ask about events in the past, and tell stories.

1 **Work in pairs. What do you think the person is reading?**

2 8.1 **Listen to the story of an invention. What is the invention?**

- **a** a television
- **b** the personal stereo
- **c** the mobile phone

3 **Do the technology quiz with your partner.**

How many times a week do you do these things?

write a letter by hand · use a mobile phone · use a computer
play computer games · use the Internet · read a book

See Vocabulary Explorer: Page 112

8A Back in the USA

Reading and listening

1 8.2 **Read and listen to the dialogue. Find three ways Brad communicated with his friends and family.**

Teacher:	OK, who's got the first question for Brad?
Julia:	Me. Brad, where did you go?
Brad:	I went to England.
Julia:	And when did you go?
Brad:	I went a year ago. I arrived in September last year.
Wayne:	Did your parents go with you?
Brad:	No, they didn't. My parents went to Antarctica for a year.
Monica:	Did you have a good time in England?
Brad:	Yes, I did. I made lots of friends.
Matt:	Did you miss your family?
Brad:	Well, it was hard at first but I saw my parents on the webcam every week. I missed my dog but my grandma emailed me photos and videos of him.
Monica:	Did you talk to your friends?
Brad:	Oh, yes. We often spoke on the computer.
Julia:	Did you take lots of things with you to England?
Brad:	No, I didn't. I took my favourite computer games and my MP3.
Wayne:	Was the food horrible?
Brad:	No, it wasn't. I didn't like English burgers. But I loved fish and chips, and Indian food.
Teacher:	And I have a question for Brad. What did you learn?
Brad:	Erm … I learned how to make a cup of English tea. My mum's English, so that's really useful!

2 Correct the mistakes in these sentences.

1. Brad went to England two years ago.
2. His parents went to England with him.
3. Brad spoke to his friends on a satellite phone.
4. He hated fish and chips.

Vocabulary

3 Work in pairs. Which activities can you do alone? In which activities do you communicate with other people? Write A (alone) or C (communicate) next to each activity.

listen to CDs
listen to an MP3
look at websites
see people on a webcam
send / receive emails
speak on a computer
use the Internet
watch videos
write / read text messages

See Vocabulary Explorer: Page 112

Grammar: past simple (questions and short answers)

4 **Complete the questions from the dialogue.**

1 Did your parents .... there?
2 Did you .... your family?
3 What did you ....?

5 **Complete the tables.**

Questions		
(**1**)	I/you/he/she/it/ we/they	like England?
Short answers		
Yes, I/you/he/she/it/we/they		did
No, I/you/he/she/it/we/they		(**2**) ....

Questions with *Wh-* words			
Where	(**3**)	I/you/he/she/it /we/they	go?

The main verb does not change in the negative and question form of the past simple.

See Grammar Explorer: Page 127

6 **Write questions with *Did*. Don't forget the prepositions!**

e.g. Brad / go / England?
Did Brad go to England?

1 he / arrive / September?
2 his suitcase / arrive / him?
3 his parents / go / London?
4 his dog / stay / the USA?
5 his friends / often talk / him?
6 he / like / English burgers?

7 **Work in pairs. Ask and answer the questions from Exercise 6.**

e.g. A: *Did Brad go to England?*
B: *Yes, he did.*

8 **Write questions about Brad with the words.**

e.g. Which city / live in?
Which city did Brad live in?

1 Who / stay with?
2 When / travel / to London?
3 Where / his parents / go?
4 Why / they / go / there?
5 What / take / to England?
6 What / learn / in England?

See Grammar Explorer: Page 127

9 **Imagine you went on a trip with your family. Choose four pictures and write sentences about the trip.**

10 **Work in pairs. Ask and answer questions about your trip.**

e.g. A: *Where did you go?*
B: *I went to …*

11 **Think of a real trip you went on with your family. Work in pairs. Ask and answer questions about your holiday.**

Fast finishers

How many answers can you think of?

(Two = good, three = excellent, four = fantastic!)

What did you read yesterday?
I read a book, …

What did you do last week?
I saw a film, …

What did you hear last night?
I heard a noise, …

Reading and listening

1 8.3 **Read and listen to the text. Which three inventions happened accidentally?**

Accidental inventions

Scientists and inventors work hard to design new things, but some great inventions happen accidentally. Three of these inventions have one thing in common – the scientists didn't try to invent them!

1 Percy Lebaron Spencer was an American engineer. In 1945, he invented the microwave oven – but he didn't try to invent it! He worked with radio signals. One day at work, a bar of chocolate in his pocket melted. Spencer experimented with different food items. The radio signals cooked them perfectly.

2 In 1968, a scientist called Spencer Silver made some new glue. It didn't stick things very well. His company didn't develop it. Seven years later, his friend thought of a use for this glue: sticky notes.

3 Sir Timothy Berners-Lee is an English computer scientist. In 1989, he developed a new communication system for computers. In 1990, he and Robert Cailliau created the World Wide Web. At the time, they didn't imagine the impact of the invention. The Web grew quickly. After a few years, it connected millions of people around the world.

4 One day in 1941, George de Mestral took his dog for a walk. Some plant seeds stuck to both of them. De Mestral didn't know why this happened. He looked at his clothes and the seeds with a microscope. Then he copied the design carefully and invented Velcro.

2 **Read the text again and answer the questions.**

1 When did Percy Lebaron Spencer invent the microwave?
2 What did Spencer Silver make in 1968?
3 Who did Sir Timothy Berners-Lee work with?
4 What is the name of George de Mestral's invention?

Listening

3 8.4 **Match the dates with the inventions and complete the sentences. Then listen to the information from a science museum and check.**

1876 1901 1957 1971 1979 1991

1 Alexander Graham Bell made the first telephone call in ....
2 A Japanese company sold the first mobile phones in ....
3 Ray Tomlinson sent the first email message in ....
4 The first webcam took pictures at Cambridge University in ....
5 Marconi sent a radio signal across the Atlantic Ocean in ....
6 Russia launched the first communications satellite in ....

Vocabulary

4 How many adverbs can you find in the text? Which adverbs are irregular?

… inventors work hard …

… some inventions happen accidentally.

Adverbs describe verbs. They usually – but not always – end in 'ly'.

See Vocabulary Explorer: Page 112

See Grammar Explorer: Page 127

5 Choose the correct adverb.

e.g. They telephoned the doctor. She came **perfectly** / **quickly** / **slowly**.

1 They had a problem. They thought **happily** / **perfectly** / **hard**.
2 The speakers were new. They worked **badly** / **clearly** / **perfectly**.
3 The printer was old. It worked **accidentally** / **quietly** / **slowly**.
4 She didn't hear the telephone because it rang **loudly** / **quietly** / **well**.
5 The keyboard was old. I used it **carefully** / **carelessly** / **perfectly**.

Grammar: past simple (negative)

6 Complete the sentence from the text. Find five more sentences with *didn't*.

The scientists .... to invent them!

7 Study the table.

Negative			
I/you/he/ she/it/we/ they	didn't (did not)	have understand	a phone. the problem.

See Grammar Explorer: Page 127

8 Make true sentences with the affirmative or negative form of the verbs.

e.g. I didn't invent the microwave oven. (**invent**)

1 Spencer Silver .... the first 'sticky notes.' (**make**)
2 George de Mestral .... a dog. (**have**)
3 Percy Lebaron Spencer .... the World Wide Web. (**design**)
4 George de Mestral .... the first microwave oven. (**develop**)
5 Sir Timothy Berners-Lee .... Velcro. (**discover**)

9 Write four sentences about what Josh didn't do yesterday.

e.g. He didn't hear his alarm clock.

1 hear / alarm clock

2 phone / school

3 read / emails

4 send / text messages

10 Work in pairs. Write four things you think your partner did yesterday. Then read your sentences to your partner and check.

e.g. A: *You got up at 7.30.*
B: *I didn't get up at 7.30. I got up at 7.35!*

Fast finishers

Find six modern communications items.

L	I	N	E	E	U	R	T	W	S
W	S	S	M	E	E	T	P	E	M
E	E	V	A	D	E	E	I	B	A
B	I	Y	I	T	U	X	L	C	S
S	U	Q	L	E	R	T	A	A	O
I	N	T	E	R	N	E	T	M	Y
T	J	E	C	I	E	G	B	M	M
E	A	B	V	I	D	E	O	T	U

8C Telling a story

Reading and listening

1 8.5 **Read and listen to the dialogue. What happened when Harry and Meera were in the shop?**

Harry: Guess what! Somebody stole my bike yesterday!
Anna: How did that happen?
Harry: Meera and I went out on our bikes yesterday morning. We stopped at the shop and bought some chocolate. I forgot to put the lock on my bike. When we came out of the shop, my bike wasn't there!
Anna: Oh, no! What did you do?
Harry: First, we looked for my bike, then I sent a text message to all the people in my phone book!
Anna: Cool!
Harry: My friends went out and looked for my bike in the streets.
Anna: But they didn't find it …
Harry: Oh yes, they did! My friend, Vivek, saw a man on my bike. He followed him to his house, then he took a photo with his phone!
Anna: Brilliant! What did your friend do then?
Harry: He sent me the picture, I told my dad and then my dad phoned the police.
Anna: Did you find your bike?
Harry: Yes. My dad went with the police to the house and they found the bike.
Anna: You were lucky!

2 **Complete the sentences with these people.**

Harry   Vivek   Harry's dad   Harry's friends

1 .... forgot to lock the bike.
2 .... looked for the bike.
3 .... found the bike.
4 .... phoned the police.
5 .... sent a text to his friends.
6 .... took a picture with a camera.

Speaking

3 **Work in pairs. A is Harry and B is Anna. Practise telling Harry's story. Use the useful expressions.**

e.g. A: *A man stole my bike!*
B: *How did it happen?*

USEFUL EXPRESSIONS

When I came out, my bike wasn't there!
First, we looked for my bike.
He followed him, then he took a photo.

4 **Work in pairs. Practise telling a story with the first line: *I lost my mobile!* Use the words in the box.**

went out / bike / yesterday
stopped / shop
went / friend's house
home / not have / mobile
went back / friend's house
mobile / not / her house
went back / shop
shop assistant / had / mobile

5 **Prepare a story. Then find a new partner and tell your story. You can use an idea from the box.**

A man stole our car.   I lost my phone.
A dog bit me.   I found some money in the street.

Pronunciation: the /ɔː/ sound

6 8.6 **Listen. What sound is in all these words? Listen again and repeat.**

bored   born   bought   call   form   four
saw   short   sport   talk   thought   walk

7 8.7 **Listen and practise these sentences. Can you say them with your eyes closed?**

1 I thought you bought some shorts.
2 We saw you walk your dog.

Writing: a story

1 **These sentences (1–6) are from a story competition. Complete the sentences with the words in the *Useful expressions* box.**

Last week, I went to my friend's house.

1 We played basketball, ... we had a pizza.
2 .... I went home, I discovered that I didn't have my house key.
3 .... I knocked on our neighbour's door, ... I phoned my mum at work.
4 .... I told her the problem, she came home.
5 .... she looked in her bag, she didn't have her key!

2 **Think of a story from your life or from a film. Write notes to answer the questions – put the verbs in the past tense. Write the story. You can add a photo or a picture.**

Where were you?
What did you do?
Who were you with?
What did you do then?
What happened?

8D Astronomers

Reading

1 Look at the photo. What can you see?

2 How much do you know about the lives of the famous astronomers Nicolaus Copernicus and Galileo Galilei? Work in pairs and do the activity. Then check the KEY.

Culture

Until about 500 years ago, people believed that the Earth was the centre of the universe. The astronomer Nicolaus Copernicus didn't accept this idea. He believed that the Sun was the centre of the solar system. Later, another astronomer, Galileo Galilei, supported this theory. Look at the mixed up information about the two astronomers' lives. Can you work out which facts are about each astronomer?

1 He wrote a book about Copernicus's ideas.
2 He lived from 1564 to 1642.
3 He made many discoveries with his telescope.
4 He said the Earth and the planets go around the Sun.
5 First he studied law, then he was interested in mathematics and astronomy.
6 He studied at the universities of Pisa and Padua.
7 He studied at the universities of Krakow and Padua.
8 He died in the same year he published his important work.
9 He wrote a book about the solar system.
10 He lived from 1473 to 1543.
11 He studied medicine, then he studied philosophy and astronomy.
12 He died after ten years of house arrest.

Nicolaus Copernicus

Galileo Galilei

Listening

3 8.8 Listen to Aesop's story of an astronomer. Put these words in the order you hear them.

e.g. 1 an old astronomer

a man his village
a deep well an old astronomer
Earth the stars in the sky

Science and English

The solar system

1 How much do you know about the solar system? Do this quiz in pairs.

2 Check your answers with your teacher.

a Put the planets in the correct order from the Sun.

e.g. Sun – Mercury – ....

Earth Jupiter Mars Mercury
Neptune Saturn Uranus Venus

b Write the name of the planet.

1 .... is 'the red planet'.
2 .... has got rings.
3 .... has got four large moons.

c Match the numbers on the diagram with the places.

Earth Moon Sun

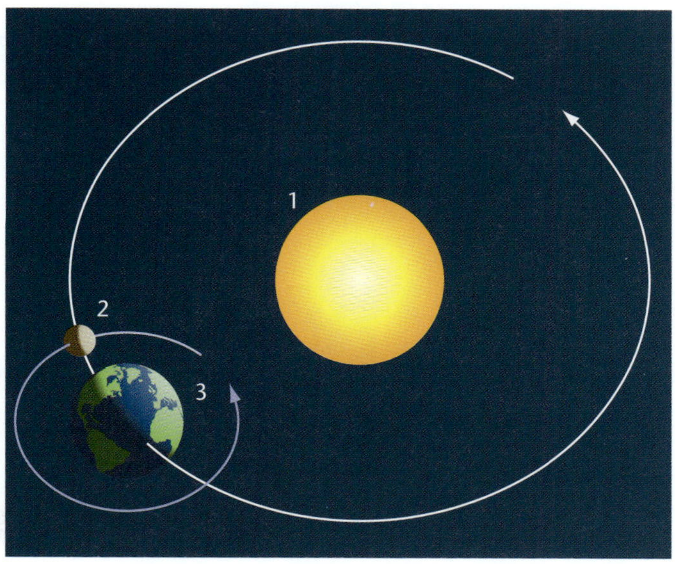

d Are the sentences true or false?

1 The Earth goes around the Sun. This takes one year.
2 The Moon goes around the Earth. This takes twenty-eight days.
3 The Earth spins on its own axis. This takes twenty-four hours.

Project

Work in pairs. Find information about a famous historical person from your country. Find a picture. Tell the class about the person's life and work.

KEY Copernicus: 4, 5, 7, 8, 9, 10; Galileo: 1, 2, 3, 6, 11, 12.

Review Units 7 and 8

Vocabulary

1 Write an adjective for each situation.

1 You got lots of presents on your birthday. You're h ....
2 You didn't eat breakfast this morning. You're h ....
3 You're going to start a new school. You're n ....
4 You're watching a film. It isn't interesting. You're b ....
5 You ate a lot of chocolates. You're i ....

1 mark per item: .../5 marks

2 Write the names of the things.

1 ....
2 ....
3 ....
4 ....
5 ....

1 mark per item: .../5 marks

3 Write the opposites.

1 go c..............
2 open c..............
3 win l..............
4 start f..............
5 take g..............

1 mark per item: .../5 marks

4 Complete the sentences with five adverbs.

accidentally carelessly carefully happily quickly quietly slowly well

1 He did his homework .... and got 1/10.
2 I can't hear her. She speaks very ....
3 You can find information .... on the Internet.
4 He speaks French .... because his mum is from France.
5 I gave him a toy and he smiled ....

1 mark per item: .../5 marks

5 Write the past simple form of these verbs.

1 drink ....
2 have ....
3 make ....
4 take ....
5 write ....

1 mark per item: .../5 marks

Grammar

6 Complete the sentences with the past simple form of *be*.

1 I .... a happy baby. (✓)
2 She .... scared of spiders. (✗)
3 We .... bored last weekend. (✓)
4 They .... nervous about the exam. (✗)
5 He .... excited about the party. (✓)

1 mark per item: .../5 marks

7 Complete the sentences with the past simple form of the verbs.

1 When I was two, I .... in York. (**live**)
2 She .... hockey after school. (**play**)
3 They .... the film. (**not like**)
4 We .... him a present (**give**)
5 I .... a text message. (**not send**)

1 mark per item: .../5 marks

8 Write past simple questions.

1 .... TV last night? (**you / watch**)
2 .... the match yesterday? (**they / win**)
3 .... late for school? (**you / be**)
4 .... breakfast at 7.00 a.m.? (**he / have**)
5 .... happy with her present? (**she / be**)

1 mark per item: .../5 marks

9 Read the answers, then complete the questions.

1 '.............. did you go you on holiday?'
'Spain.'
2 '.............. was the baby's christening?'
'In May.'
3 '.............. did you stay with?'
'My aunt and uncle.'
4 '.............. did you have for lunch?'
'Salad and an orange.'
5 '.............. did you lose your mobile?'
'I left it in a shop.'

1 mark per item: .../5 marks

10 Complete the sentences.

1 I went to Greece .... 2005.
2 When .... you start school?
3 .... was your first teacher?
4 What did you do .... night?
5 His parents got married fifteen years ....

1 mark per item: .../5 marks

Communicate

11 Choose the correct response.

1 Would you like to play tennis tomorrow?
  a I'm sorry, I can't. **b** At seven o'clock.
  c No, I'm not.
2 Hello, can I speak to Jill, please?
  a No, she isn't. **b** Yes, who is it?
  c It's Mark.
3 Do you want to go to the beach tomorrow?
  a Would you like to come?
  b I want to.
  c Thanks, I'd love to.
4 It's my birthday.
  a Good luck! **b** Happy Birthday!
  c Congratulations!
5 Where's the party?
  a On Saturday. **b** At our house.
  c At half past eight.

2 marks per item: .../10 marks

12 Choose the correct sound for each verb ending.

1 arrived /t/ /d/ /ɪd/
2 celebrated /t/ /d/ /ɪd/
3 climbed /t/ /d/ /ɪd/
4 cooked /t/ /d/ /ɪd/
5 helped /t/ /d/ /ɪd/
6 invited /t/ /d/ /ɪd/
7 opened /t/ /d/ /ɪd/
8 looked /t/ /d/ /ɪd/
9 travelled /t/ /d/ /ɪd/
10 worked /t/ /d/ /ɪd/

1 mark per item: .../10 marks

13 Complete the dialogue with the questions.

Did you find it? Where did you look? What did you do? How did that happen? What did your mum do?

Jill: I lost my phone yesterday.
Mark: **(1)** ....
Jill: I was late for school and I forgot to close my bag.
Mark: **(2)** ....
Jill: I looked for it!
Mark: **(3)** ....
Jill: In the garden and at the bus stop.
Mark: **(4)** ....
Jill: No.
Mark: **(5)** ....
Jill: She phoned the bus company. The bus driver had it!

2 marks per item: .../10 marks

14 Put the sentences in the correct order to tell the story. The first one is given.

1 ......f...... 2 .... 3 .... 4 .... 5 .... 6 ....

a First, the doctor cleaned my finger.
b My parents took me to the doctor.
c One day, the parrot bit my finger.
d Then she gave me an injection.
e The injection hurt more than the parrot's bite!
f When I was a child, we had a parrot.

2 marks per item: .../10 marks

15 Complete the invitation with these words.

a at at can celebrate come in like on week

Dear Mark,

It's Halloween next **(1)** .... We're going to have a bonfire party **(2)** .... Friday. Would you **(3)** .... to come and **(4)** .... with us? You **(5)** .... wear fancy dress. The theme is vampires! The party's **(6)** .... our cousin's house **(7)** .... 8.00 p.m. He lives in Stanhope Street, **(8)** .... the first house. Bring **(9)** .... friend! We hope you can **(10)** ....

Jill and Kelly

1 mark per item: .../10 marks

Total: .../100

I can...

I can talk about events in the past.
I can make, accept and decline invitations.
I can ask about events in the past.
I can tell stories.

1 Vocabulary Explorer

Family relationships

1	grandfather	9	brother
2	grandmother	10	sister
3	grandparents	11	cousin
4	father	12	son
5	mother	13	daughter
6	parents	14	children
7	aunt	15	niece
8	uncle	16	nephew

1 VE1 **Listen and repeat.**

2 VE2 **Cover the word box. Listen and say the number.**

3 **Work in pairs.**

A: Say a family relationship.

B: Cover the the word box. Say the number.

e.g. **A:** *brother*

B: *9*

Take turns.

Appearance

1	tall	7	old
2	short	8	young
3	fat	9	fair
4	thin	10	dark
5	happy	11	blond
6	sad	12	red-haired

1 VE3 **Listen and repeat.**

2 VE4 **Cover the word box. Listen and say the number.**

3 **Work in pairs.**

A: Say a number.

B: Cover the word box. Say the adjective.

e.g. **A:** *8*

B: *young*

Take turns.

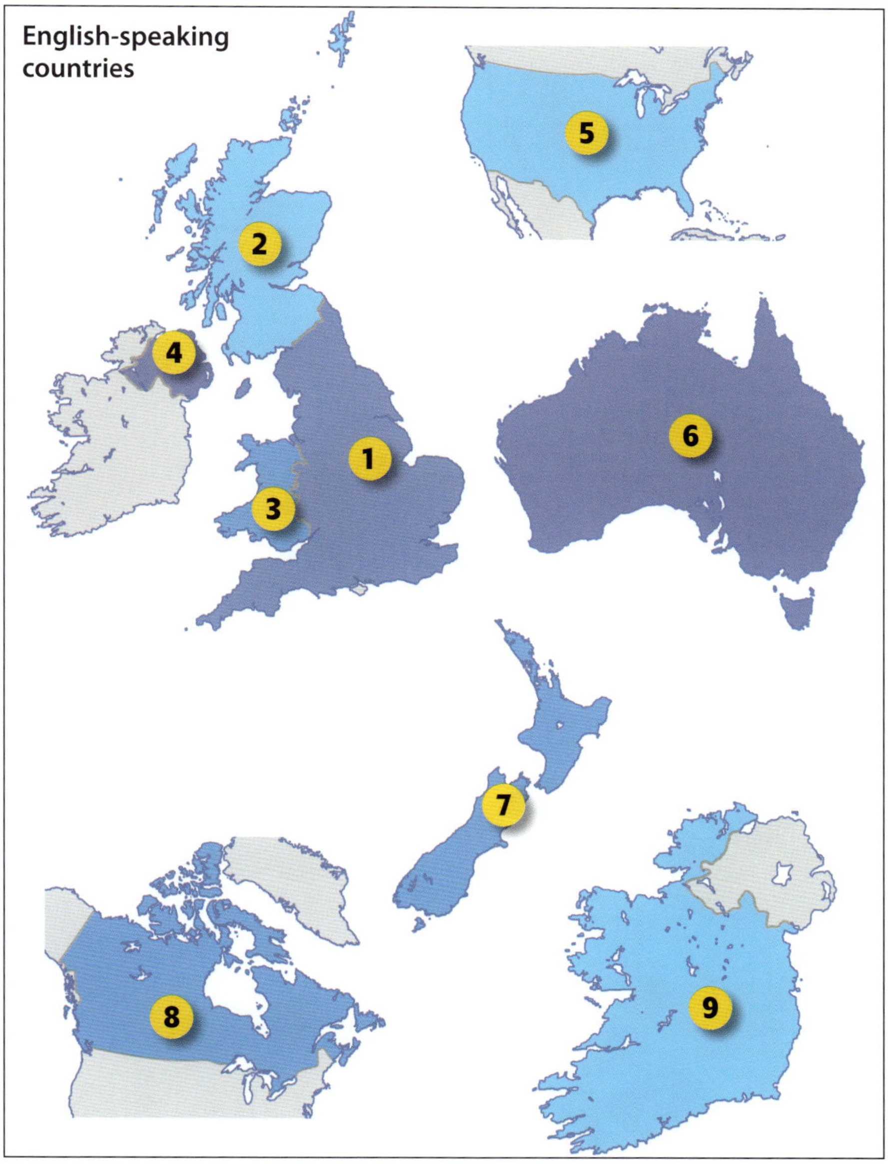

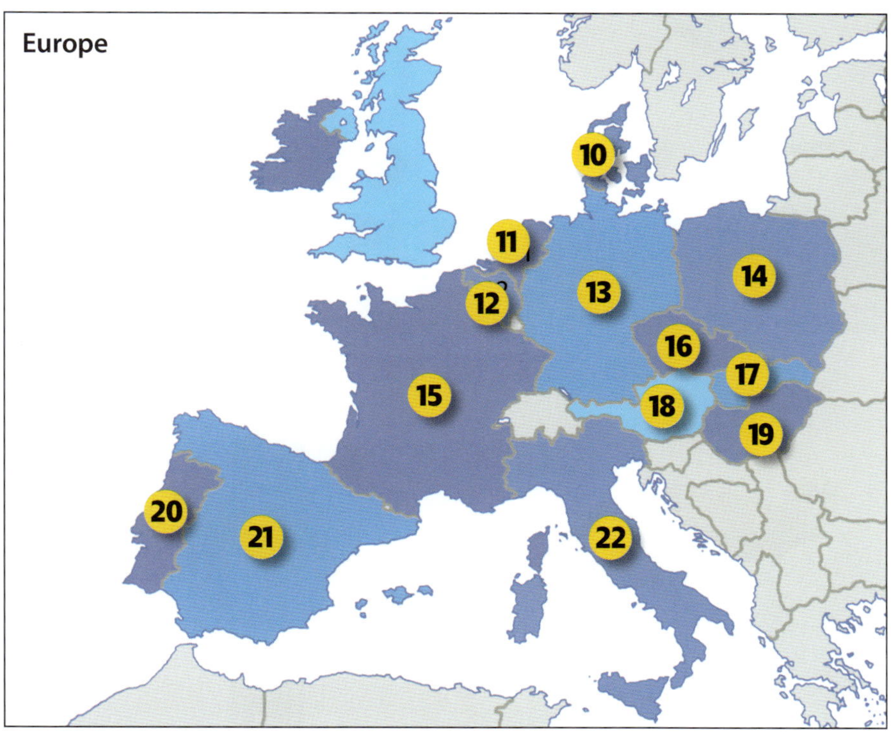

Countries

1 England
2 Scotland
3 Wales
4 Northern Ireland
5 the United States
6 Australia
7 New Zealand
8 Canada
9 Ireland
10 Denmark
11 Holland
12 Belgium
13 Germany
14 Poland
15 France
16 Czech Republic
17 Slovakia
18 Austria
19 Hungary
20 Portugal
21 Spain
22 Italy

1 VE5 **Listen and repeat.**

2 VE6 **Cover the word box. Listen and say the number.**

3 **Work in pairs.**

A: Say a country.
B: Cover the word box. Say the number.

e.g. **A:** *Australia*
B: *6*

Take turns.

2 Vocabulary Explorer

Possessions

1 a photo album
2 a bag
3 a camera
4 a car
5 a comic
6 a computer
7 a key
8 a mobile phone
9 an MP3
10 a purse
11 a radio
12 a toy
13 a travel card
14 an umbrella
15 a watch

1 VE7 **Listen and repeat.**

2 VE8 **Cover the word box. Listen and say the number.**

3 **Work in pairs.**

A: Say a possession.
B: Cover the word box. Say the number.

e.g. A: a camera
B: 3

Take turns.

1

2

3

4

5

6

7

8

9
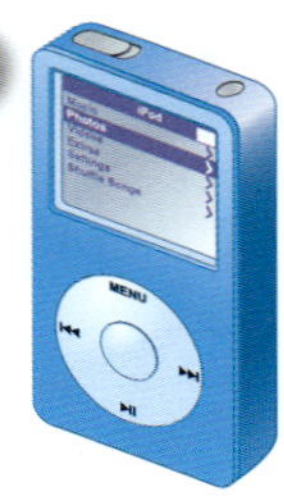

10

11
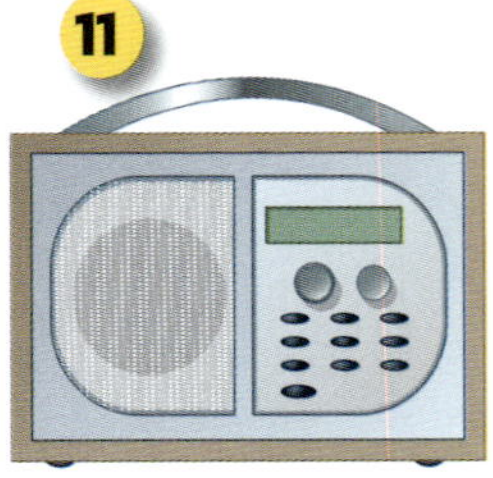

12

13

14

15

Skills and abilities

1 climb
2 cook
3 copy a CD
4 drive
5 fight
6 fly
7 jump
8 make things
9 play tennis
10 play the piano
11 send an email
12 speak Spanish
13 swim
14 use the Internet

1 VE9 **Listen and repeat.**

2 VE10 **Cover the word box. Listen and say the number.**

3 **Work in pairs.**

A: Say a number.
B: Cover the word box. Say the activity.

e.g. **A:** *13*
B: *swim*

Take turns.

1

2

3

4

5

6

7

8

9

10

11

12

13

14

3 Vocabulary Explorer

School subjects

1	art	7	history
2	biology	8	IT
3	chemistry	9	maths
4	English	10	PE
5	French	11	physics
6	geography	12	music

1 VE11 **Listen and repeat.**

2 VE12 **Cover the word box. Listen and say the number.**

3 Work in pairs.

A: Say a number.

B: Cover the word box. Say the school subject.

e.g. A: *9*

B: *maths*

Take turns.

Interests and activities

1 animals
2 cycling
3 dancing
4 drawing and painting
5 fashion
6 films
7 music
8 reading
9 sports
10 shopping
11 singing
12 sleeping

1 VE13 **Listen and repeat.**

2 VE14 **Cover the word box. Listen and say the number.**

3 Work in pairs.

A: Say a word.

B: Cover the word box. Say the number.

e.g. A: *music*

B: *7*

Take turns.

Food

1 bananas
2 bread
3 butter
4 cakes
5 carrots
6 cheese
7 chicken
8 chocolate
9 curry
10 fish
11 ice cream
12 meat
13 milk
14 pasta
15 pizza
16 potatoes
17 rice
18 sausages
19 strawberries
20 yoghurt

1 VE15 **Listen and repeat.**

2 VE16 **Cover the word box. Listen and say the number.**

3 **Work in pairs.**

A: Say a number.
B: Cover the word box. Say the food item.

e.g. **A:** *16*
B: *potatoes*

Take turns.

4 Vocabulary Explorer

Sports

1 athletics
2 basketball
3 boxing
4 diving
5 football
6 gymnastics
7 hockey
8 running
9 skating
10 skiing
11 tennis
12 volleyball

1 VE17 **Listen and repeat.**

2 VE18 **Cover the word box. Listen and say the number.**

3 **Work in pairs.**

A: Say a number.
B: Cover the word box. Say the sport.

e.g. A: *8*
B: *diving*

Take turns.

Daily routine

1 get up
2 get dressed
3 have breakfast
4 brush your teeth
5 leave the house
6 have lunch
7 arrive home
8 do homework
9 have dinner
10 have a bath
11 have a shower
12 go to bed

1 VE19 **Listen and repeat.**

2 VE20 **Cover the word box. Listen and say the number.**

3 **Work in pairs.**

A: Say an activity.
B: Cover the word box. Say the number.

e.g. **A:** *brush your teeth*
B: *4*

Take turns.

5 Vocabulary Explorer

House and furniture

1 the bathroom
2 the bedroom
3 the study
4 the kitchen
5 the living room
6 the garage
7 the garden
8 a bath
9 a bed
10 a bin
11 a chair
12 a chest of drawers
13 a cupboard
14 a desk
15 a dishwasher
16 a fridge
17 a ceiling light
18 a microwave
19 a rug
20 shelves
21 a shower
22 a sofa
23 a table
24 a wardrobe
25 a washing machine

1 VE21 **Listen and repeat.**

2 VE22 **Cover the word box. Listen and say the number.**

3 **Work in pairs.**

A: Say a number.
B: Cover the word box. Say the room or item of furniture.

e.g. **A:** *8*
B: *a bath*

Take turns.

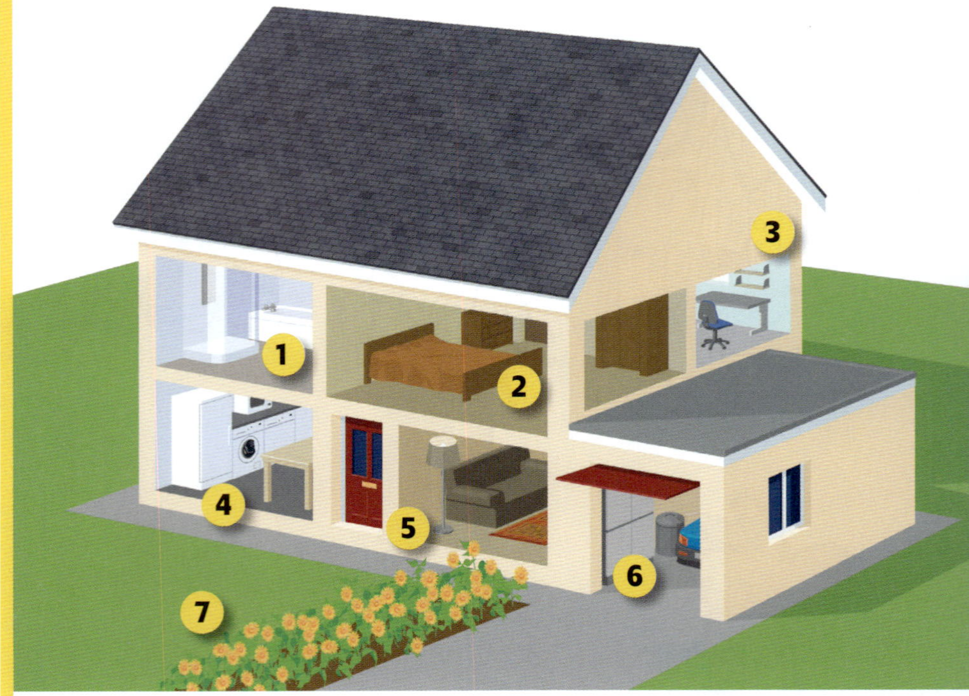

Natural features

1 a beach
2 a desert
3 a field
4 ice
5 a lake
6 a mountain
7 a path
8 a river
9 the sea
10 snow
11 a tree

1 VE23 **Listen and repeat.**

2 VE24 **Cover the word box. Listen and say the number.**

3 **Work in pairs.**

A: Say a natural feature.
B: Cover the word box. Say the word.

e.g. **A:** *a river*
B: *8*

Take turns.

1

2

3

4

5

6

7

8

9

10

11

6 Vocabulary Explorer

Clothes

1 boots
2 a cap
3 a coat
4 a dress
5 gloves
6 a jacket
7 jeans
8 sandals
9 a scarf
10 a shirt
11 shoes
12 shorts
13 a skirt
14 socks
15 sunglasses
16 a sweatshirt
17 a top
18 trainers
19 trousers
20 a T-shirt

1 VE25 **Listen and repeat.**

2 VE26 **Cover the word box. Listen and say the number.**

3 **Work in pairs.**

A: Say a clothes item.
B: Cover the word box. Say the number.

e.g. **A:** *a top*
B: *17*

Take turns.

Places in a town

1 a bank
2 a church
3 a cinema
4 a museum
5 a park
6 a post office
7 a restaurant
8 a shop
9 a sports centre
10 a supermarket

1 VE27 **Listen and repeat.**

2 VE28 **Cover the word box. Listen and say the number.**

3 **Work in pairs.**

A: Say a number.
B: Cover the word box. Say the place.

e.g. **A:** *8*
B: *a shop*

Take turns.

7 Vocabulary Explorer

Adjectives

1 bored
2 excited
3 happy
4 hungry
5 ill
6 nervous
7 scared
8 tired

1 VE29 **Listen and repeat.**

2 VE30 **Cover the word box. Listen and say the name.**

3 **Work in pairs.**

A: Say a name.
B: Cover the word box. Say the adjective.

e.g. **A:** *Lily*
B: *bored*

Take turns.

1 Lily

2 Natalie

3 Arthur

4 George

5 Toby

6 James

7 Jenni

8 Ralph

Irregular verbs

1 see saw
Josh **saw** his friends at school.

2 give gave
He **gave** his friends an invitation to his birthday party.

3 read read
His friends **read** the invitation.

4 buy bought
His sister **bought** a present.

5 make made
His mum **made** a cake.

6 say said
His sister **said** 'Happy Birthday'.

7 begin began
The party **began** at seven o'clock.

8 come came
His friends **came** to the party.

9 drink drank
His brother **drank** fruit juice.

10 eat ate
They **ate** some cake.

11 take took
His mum **took** some photos.

12 go went
His friends **went** home at half past nine.

13 have had
Josh **had** a great time.

14 win won
His brother **won** every game.

15 write wrote
He **wrote** 'thank-you' letters to his friends.

1 VE31 **Listen and repeat.**

2 VE32 **Listen and say the past tense.**

3 **Work in pairs.**

A: Say a verb.

B: Cover the word box. Point to the picture and say the past tense. Can you remember the sentence too?

e.g. A: begin

B: began

Take turns.

8 Vocabulary Explorer

Technology

1 a computer
2 a keyboard
3 a mouse
4 a pendrive
5 a printer
6 a screen
7 speakers
8 a webcam

1 VE33 **Listen and repeat.**

2 VE34 **Cover the word box. Listen and say the number.**

3 **Work in pairs.**

A: Say a word.
B: Cover the word box. Say the number.

e.g. A: *a mouse*
B: *3*

Take turns.

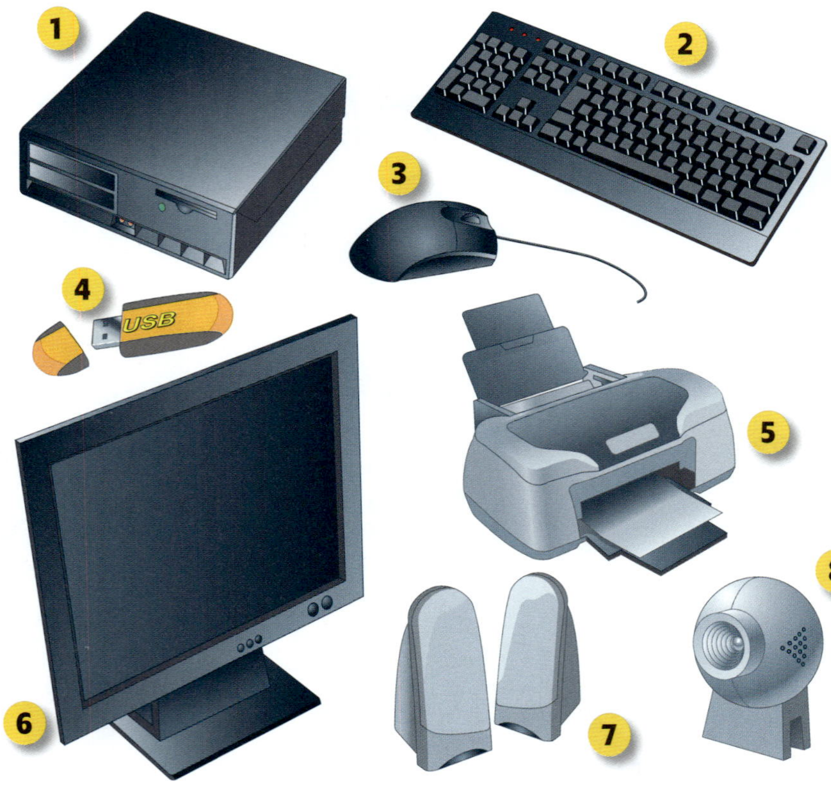

Adverbs

1 badly
2 carelessly
3 happily
4 loudly
5 quickly
6 quietly
7 slowly
8 well

1 VE35 **Listen and repeat.**

2 VE36 **Cover the word box. Listen and say the number.**

3 **Work in pairs.**

A: Say a number.
B: Cover the word box. Say the word.

e.g. A: *2*
B: *carelessly*

Take turns.

1

2

3

4
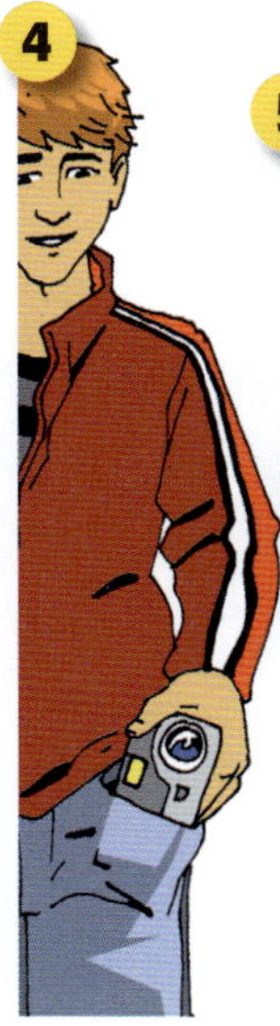

5

6

7

8

9

10

11

12

Irregular verbs

1 find found
He **found** some keys.

2 leave left
She **left** home.

3 lose lost
She **lost** her purse.

4 put put
He **put** his camera in his pocket.

5 sell sold
She **sold** some apples.

6 send sent
She **sent** a letter.

7 speak spoke
He **spoke** on his mobile.

8 steal stole
She **stole** an apple.

9 stick stuck
He **stuck** the note on the screen.

10 think thought
She **thought** of a name.

11 tell told
He **told** the police officer what happened.

12 understand understood
They **understood** the maths lesson.

1 VE37 **Listen and repeat.**

2 VE38 **Listen and say the past tense.**

3 **Work in pairs.**

A: Say a verb.
B: Cover the word box. Point to the picture and say the past tense. Can you remember the sentence too?

e.g. **A:** *tell*
B: *told*

Take turns.

VIDEO WORKSHEET

1 Happy elephants

How can people keep elephants happy in zoos? Mike Hackenberger is an elephant trainer. His elephants are very healthy and he talks to them. In the past, people in zoos were not good to animals. Now they try to make them happy.

Before you watch

1 You are going to watch a film about elephants. Check you understand the words below.

wild captivity zoo circus feeling healthy happy herd

Do you think elephants can be happy? Watch the film to find out.

While you watch

PART ONE: Elephants and people

2 Listen and repeat these words.

zoo happy animals

Now watch the first part of the film, and write the words in the gaps.

1 Elephants are very large ...., but they are also gentle and intelligent.
2 Mike Hackenberger is an animal trainer at Baltimore ....
3 His elephants are very healthy and seem to be ....

PART TWO: Do elephants have feelings?

3 Listen and repeat these words.

families wild feelings

Now watch the second part of the film, and complete the sentences.

1 Can elephants be happy? Do animals have ....?
2 Elephants are happy if their home in the zoo or circus is similar to their life in the ....
3 Elephants live in .... and herds, and they need other elephants.

PART THREE: How to be elephants

4 Listen and repeat these words.

young learn alone

Now watch the third part of the film, and write the words in the gaps.

1 Limba was .... for 30 years in a zoo in Northern Quebec.
2 Limba fell in love with the two .... elephants.
3 Elephants need to .... how to be elephants.

After you watch

5 Now read the introduction and watch the whole film. Are the sentences true (T) or false (F)?

1 Elephants with people are usually in zoos or circuses. **T / F**
2 Mike Hackenberger thinks his elephants are unhappy. **T / F**
3 Elephants are happy if their home is in the zoo or a circus. **T / F**
4 It is important that elephants live alone. **T / F**
5 Hackenberger lets elephants do the things they do naturally in the wild. **T / F**

6 Watch the film again. Put the words in the correct order to make sentences.

1 in captivity. / When they are with people, / elephants are usually

....

2 elephants have feelings. / say 'yes' / who work with animals / Many people

....

3 when she was alone. / was not at all happy / Limba

....

4 that elephants need to learn / how to be elephants. / Hackenberger believes

....

VIDEO WORKSHEET

2 Knife markets of Sanaa

Sanaa is a beautiful old city in the Middle East. It is the capital of Yemen. Jambiya are beautiful traditional knives. There are always a lot of knives in the souqs (markets) of Sanaa. But the handles are made from rhinoceros horn, and this is illegal.

Before you watch

1 You are going to watch a video about a traditional knife called a *jambiya*. Jambiya come from Yemen. Check that you understand the words below.

knife blade handle weapon souq
belt rhinoceros horn

While you watch

PART ONE: The souq

2 Listen and repeat these words.

status symbol jambiya weapon souqs city

Now watch the first part of the film, and write the words in the gaps.

1 Sanaa is the capital .... of Yemen.
2 There are busy .... in the streets of Sanaa.
3 A .... is a large, beautifully decorated knife.
4 These days, people don't use the jambiya as a ....
5 The jambiya is a .... and sign of Yemeni manhood.

PART TWO: The problem with tradition

3 Listen and repeat these words.

rhinoceros horn handle government
prices problem

Now watch the second part of the film, and complete the sentences.

1 The .... are different for each jambiya.
2 The value of a knife depends on the ....
3 Yemeni knife makers use .... for the handle.
4 The jambiya is part of a big .... the illegal killing of rhinos.
5 The Yemeni .... is trying to stop people illegally buying and selling rhinoceros horn.

After you watch

4 Now read the introduction and watch the whole film. Are the sentences true or false?

1 The day begins in Sanaa with the call to prayer. **T / F**
2 The tall houses of Sanaa are made of ginger bread. **T / F**
3 You can buy jewellery and spices in the markets (souqs). **T / F**
4 Yemeni women wear the jambiya in a special belt. **T / F**
5 A traditional jambiya has got a rhino horn handle. **T / F**
6 The Yemeni government can stop the illegal killing of rhinos. **T / F**
7 The government wants people to use different materials for jambiya handles. **T / F**

5 Watch the film again. Choose the correct word to complete the sentences.

1 Sanaa is an ancient **souq / city / house**.
2 Some people think the **souqs / streets / houses** look like gingerbread.
3 The **children /men / women** in Yemen have got special knives.
4 The men wear the jambiya in a special **blade / knife / belt**.
5 Today, the jambiya is a **weapon / status symbol / belt**.
6 The **handles / blades / belts** of the knives are made of rhinoceros horn.
7 The **handle / blade / knife** of the jambiya is hooked.
8 In Yemen it is a **tradition / idea / weapon** to use rhinoceros horn for jambiya handles.

VIDEO WORKSHEET

3 Dreamtime painters

In Australia there are some very old rock paintings. They are 30,000 years old. The paintings are of the 'dreamtime' – the story of the beginning of the world. The Aboriginal people are a very old civilisation. They have lived in Australia for 40,000 years, perhaps more.

Before you watch

1 Check you understand the words below.

art / artist   to paint / painter / paint / painting
rock   dreamtime   civilisation

While you watch

PART ONE: The rock paintings of Kakadu National Park

2 Listen and repeat these words.

artists   traditional   paintings   dreamtime

Now watch the first part of the film, and write the words in the gaps.

1 The rock .... are more than 30,000 years old.
2 The .... is the story of the beginning of the world.
3 The dreamtime paintings are by Aboriginal ....
4 Thompson Yulidgirru is an artist who still paints in the .... Aboriginal way.

PART TWO: An ancient civilization

3 Listen and repeat these words.

fish x2   civilisation   power   animals

Now watch the second part of the film, and complete the sentences.

1 The Aboriginal people are the oldest human .... on earth.
2 The Aboriginal people believed that the paintings had special ....
3 If they painted a lot of ...., they would catch a lot of ....
4 Certain groups painted certain ....

PART THREE: Aboriginal art today

4 Listen and repeat these words.

colour   paper   problem

Now watch the third part of the film, and complete the sentences.

1 Today, Aboriginal artists paint on bark, ... and wood.
2 Unfortunately, there is a .... with the original rock paintings.
3 The paintings are losing their .... because of time and bad weather.

After you watch

5 Read the introduction and watch the whole film again. Match the beginning of each sentence with the end.

1 Australia is ...
2 Ian Morris is ...
3 The Kakadu National Park is ...
4 Long ago, the Aboriginal people believed ...
5 One piece of Aboriginal art ...
6 Unfortunately, there is ...
7 If a group painted turtles, ...

a a naturalist who has lived most of his life in Australia.
b can now cost tens of thousands of Australian dollars.
c a very large country with a varied landscape.
d that's the only thing they painted.
e that the paintings had special power.
f now a problem with the original rock paintings.
g owned by the Aboriginal people.

VIDEO WORKSHEET

4 Alaskan ice climbing

People go to Alaska to climb mountains and glaciers and to ski on them. The weather changes a lot, and so a group of climbers decide to climb a glacier instead of skiing down a mountain.

Before you watch

1 Match the weather words with the symbols.

cloud fog rain snow wind

While you watch

PART ONE: Climbing school in Alaska

2 Listen and repeat these words.

climbing weather glacier

Now watch the first part of the film, and complete the sentences.

1 The group of visitors want to fly to a .... and ski down it.
2 The group of visitors can't go out today because the .... is bad.
3 Caitlin and Colby Coombs have got a .... school.

PART TWO: A new plan

3 Listen and repeat these words.

hike climb ice icefall

Now watch the second part of the film, and complete the sentences.

1 The group won't ski down a glacier – it will .... up one.
2 The Matanuska glacier is a 30-foot wall of ....
3 The .... across Matanuska is beautiful but it can be dangerous.
4 The climbers must be careful – they could easily .... in.

PART THREE: At the heart of the glacier

4 Listen and repeat these words.

seracs icefall view lake

Now watch the third part of the film, and complete the sentences.

1 At the heart of the glacier, there's a beautiful ....
2 There's a glacial .... with many seracs.
3 .... are large pieces of blue glacial ice that stick up in the air
4 An area with many seracs is called an ....

After you watch

5 Read the introduction again and watch the whole film. Are the sentences true or false?

1 The weather in Alaska changes all the time. **T / F**
2 They can't fly to the mountain because of low clouds. **T / F**
3 Colby and Caitlin are often worried in the mountains, because it's very dangerous there. **T / F**
4 The Matanuska glacier is 20,000 years old. **T / F**
5 One summer, a young woman fell into an opening in the ice and died. **T / F**
6 An ice fall is an area with many seracs. **T / F**

6 Watch the film again. Put the words in order to make the questions for the answers below.

1 does the group / want to do? / of visitors / What
They want to fly onto a glacier and ski down it.
2 Denali? / is / What
It's a mountain – the highest mountain in North America.
3 when they / get to the top of the glacier? / How / feel / do the climbers
They feel great.
4 glaciers / in Alaska? / are there / How many *100,000.*

VIDEO WORKSHEET

5 Don't believe your eyes!

Camogli is a fishing village in Italy. Many of the houses in Camogli have windows and stonework that are not real. There is a local tradition of trompe l'oeil – paintings that look real. Now there are only a few artists who can still paint in the trompe l'oeil tradition.

Before you watch

1 Check you understand the words below.

art / artist   to paint / painter / paint / painting
stone / stonework   building

2 You are going to watch a video about a style of painting called *trompe l'oeil*. What kind of paintings do you think you are going to see?

While you watch

PART ONE: A small fishing village

3 Listen and repeat these words.

art   stonework (x2)   real

Now watch the first part of the film, and complete the sentences.

1 In the town of Camogli, there are many things that seem ...., but they are not.
2 *Trompe l'oeil* is a type of .... where nothing is what it seems to be.
3 There seems to be detailed ...., but it isn't .... – it's paint!

PART TWO: The trompe l'oeil tradition

4 Listen and repeat these words.

paint   artists   stone

Now watch the second part of the film, and complete the sentences.

1 The fisherman of Camogli liked to .... their houses in bright colours.
2 Today, only a few .... still paint *trompe l'oeil* houses.
3 There is one .... course at the Palazzo Spinelli Art School in Florence.

PART THREE: Carlo Pere – a trompe l'oeil artist

5 Listen and repeat these words.

traditions   business   history

Now watch the third part of the film, and complete the sentences.

1 Carlo Pere studied *trompe l'oeil*. Now he's made a .... of it.
2 Carlo's style comes from .... He uses an art book from the 1300s.
3 He wants to protect the *trompe l'oeil* ....

After you watch

6 Now read the introduction and watch the whole film again. Put the words in order to make sentences.

1 very interesting. / you'll see something / But, if you look carefully,
....
2 – in solid walls. / in this particular village / For example, / you see windows open
....
3 to make simple buildings / This style of art / look grand and expensive. / is a way
....
4 that it looks real. / to paint stone so well / to learn / Rafaella worked for 20 years
....
5 a new place. / Carlo thinks / something unexpected to / that *trompe l'oeil* brings
....
6 from the 1300s / to study the technique. / an art book / He uses
....

VIDEO WORKSHEET

6 The story of the Hula

In Hawaii there is a special traditional dance called the Hula. Dancers imitate the waves of the sea with their hands. For a long time, people were not allowed to dance the Hula in public. Now, a lot of people learn the Hula and there is an important Hula competition in Hilo.

Before you watch

1 You are going to watch a video about the Hula, a Hawaiian dance. Check that you understand these words.

traditional ban clothes religious secret

Work in pairs. Talk about what you think is the link between these words.

While you watch

PART ONE: A Hawaiian dance

2 Listen and repeat these words.

islands dance waves

Now watch the first part of the film, and complete the sentences.

1 Hawaii is a group of beautiful tropical ....
2 A special .... called the Hula started in Hawaii 300 years ago.
3 The dancers imitated the .... with their hands.

PART TWO: The Hula now and in the past

3 Listen and repeat these words.

ban secret schools culture religious

Now watch the second part of the film, and complete the sentences.

1 The .... people were surprised by the Hula.
2 They asked the queen of Hawaii to .... the dance.
3 The dancers danced the Hula in ....
4 Now there is a new interest in Hawaiian ....
5 Hulaus are .... that teach the dance in a traditional way.

PART THREE: The competition in Hilo

4 Listen and repeat these words.

skirt competition life judges

Now watch the third part of the film, and complete the sentences.

1 The most important Hula .... happens in Hilo, Hawaii.
2 In the competition, the .... look at more than just the dance.
3 The judges look at the way a person wears a .... and the colour of their costume.
4 Today in Hawaii, the Hula is once again part of everyday ....

5 Now read the introduction and watch the whole film. Look back at your answer to question 1. Were you right?

After you watch

6 Watch the whole film again. Are the sentences true or false?

1 The Hula is more than three thousand years old. T / F
2 Hula dancers did not wear many clothes. T / F
3 Religious people asked the king of Hawaii to ban the dance. T / F
4 Hulaus are schools that teach religion. T / F
5 It's not difficult to learn the Hula. T / F
6 Today many Hawaiians don't speak the language. T / F
7 Hulau students practice the Hula for many hours. T / F
8 In the competition, the judges look at more than just the dance. T / F

VIDEO WORKSHEET

7 Young riders of Mongolia

Mongolia has a long tradition of riding horses. In the festival of Naadam, there is a horse race. All of the riders are under 12 years old. 500 young riders race their horses to a big stadium. The winners get a blue sash and a medal.

Before you watch

1 **You are going to watch a video about a special horse race in Mongolia. Check that you understand the words below. Which word is the odd one out?**

horse to ride / rider race to win / winner
parents to compete/competition

While you watch

PART ONE: The Naadam race

2 **Listen and repeat these words.**

horses race riding riders

Now watch the first part of the film, and complete the sentences.

1 Mongolian people are very good at horse ....
2 Many people need .... for their everyday life.
3 But the Naadam .... is a bit different.
4 The .... must be less than twelve years old.

PART TWO: Before the race

3 **Listen and repeat these words.**

milk incense leather preparations

Now watch the second part of the film, and complete the sentences.

1 On the day of the first race, ... begin early in the morning.
2 The racers cover each horse's tail with ....
3 They use .... to clean the area around the rider of bad spirits.
4 Finally, a drop of .... near the legs keeps the riders and their horses safe.

PART THREE : The young riders

4 **Listen and repeat these words.**

sash finish medals

Now watch the third part of the film, and complete the sentences.

1 People wait at the .... line but they can't see the riders.
2 The first five horses get a blue .... for winning.
3 The winners get .... and horse's milk.

5 **Now read the introduction again and watch the whole film. What is special about the Naadam race?**

After you watch

6 **Watch the whole film again. Put the words in the correct order to make sentences.**

1 days of / In the / Genghis Khan, / Mongolia had / a very strong army

....

2 build / helped him to / In the 1200s / the army / one of the largest empires ever.

....

3 less than / must be / the Naadam race / The riders in / twelve years old.

....

4 early in the morning. / of the race, / On the day / preparations begin

....

5 safe. / keeps the horses and riders / near the legs / People think that / a drop of milk

....

6 about five hundred riders / first race. / in the / There were

....

VIDEO WORKSHEET

8 Snow magic

Dan Raedeke owns a ski business in Minnesota. He likes to open the ski area in November, but there isn't always enough snow. He uses snow machines to make snow. It takes a lot of skill and hard work to make good snow for skiing.

Before you watch

1 You are going to watch a video about a man who makes snow. Check you understand the words below.

snow freeze temperature pipe pump reservoir trail

While you watch

PART ONE: Wild Mountain ski area

2 Listen and repeat these words.

snow-making snow air weather

Now watch the first part of the film, and complete the sentences.

1 Dan Raedeke doesn't like warm .... in the winter.
2 He needs .... for his business.
3 Raedeke owns the largest .... system in the area.
4 He needs to carefully watch the water, the .... temperature and the wind direction.

PART TWO: The snow-making machines

3 Listen and repeat these words.

water sticks machines man-made trails

Now watch the second part of the film, and complete the sentences.

1 There are good things about real snow, and there are good things about .... snow.
2 Raedeke's newest .... are tall, thin poles called water sticks.
3 There are always .... on half of the Wild Mountain trails
4 On the other ...., there are the very big snow guns.

PART THREE: Snow making needs lots of water

4 Listen and repeat these words.

reservoir night pumps pipe

Now watch the third part of the film, and complete the sentences.

1 The six .... in the building control the water.
2 If a .... freezes, then you can't use it for the rest of the winter.
3 The .... provides 3,000 gallons of water per minute for the system.
4 To prepare for the next day, Raedeke operates the snow machines all ....

After you watch

5 Now read the introduction and watch the whole film again. Are the sentences true or false?

1 Dan Raedeke doesn't like warm weather in winter. T / F
2 Raedeke likes to open the ski area in December. T / F
3 Raedeke's family own Wild Mountain ski area. T / F
4 Raedeke studied mechanical engineering. T / F
5 Man-made snow is drier, softer and better quality for skiing. T / F
6 Water sticks can produce a lot of snow quickly. T / F
7 There are water sticks on all the Wild Mountain trails. T / F
8 The reservoir provides 3,000 gallons of water every minute for the snow-making system. T / F

Grammar Explorer

Unit 1

be (affirmative)

The present simple of ***be*** has three forms: ***am***, ***are*** and ***is***.

I am a boy. ***You/We/They are students.*** ***He/She/It is old.***

In English, we use ***you*** for one person (singular) or for lots of people (plural). The verb form for ***you*** singular and ***you*** plural is always the same.

We use ***be*** to talk about names, ages, nationalities, jobs, etc. We also use ***be*** to describe people and things.

I am Susan. I am thirteen.
You are a good student. You are very clever.
You are my friends.
We are sisters.
They are English.
Brad is a basketball player. He is tall and thin.
She is my cousin. She is dark-haired.
The suitcase is from America. It is blue.

We use the **short form** in everyday language.

Long form							
I am	you are	he is	she is	it is	we are	you are	they are
Short form							
I'm	you're	he's	she's	it's	we're	you're	they're

Hi – I'm Harry. You're funny! He's at school. We're fourteen.

Affirmative		
I'm (I am) You're (You are) He's (He is) She's (She is) It's (It is)	We're (We are) You're (You are) They're (They are)	from America.

be (negative)

We make the negative of ***be*** by adding the word ***not*** after ***am/ are/is***.

Notice the short form of ***are*** and ***is*** in the negative:
I'm not ***You/We/They aren't*** ***He/She/It isn't***

Negative	
I'm not (am not) You/We/They aren't (are not) He/She/It isn't (is not)	a basketball player. very happy. from France.

be (questions and short answers)

We make questions by putting ***am/are/is*** before the subject (*I, you/we/they, he/she/it*).

We don't use short forms (*I'm, you're*, etc) with affirmative short answers.

Questions	
Am I Are you/we/they Is he/she/it	from America?
Short answers	
Yes, I am. Yes, you/we/they are. Yes, he/she/it is.	No, I'm not. No, you/we/they aren't. No, he/she/it isn't.

Possessive adjectives

We use a **possessive adjective** before a noun to say who/what it belongs to or is related to.

I'm from France. My home is in Paris.
He's red-haired. His hair is red.
She's my grandmother. Her son is my dad.
We're students. Our teacher is Miss Stanton.
They're my friends. Their names are Becky and Tom.

Be careful with these words:
you're (you are) and *your* — ***If you're hungry, here's your food.***
it's (it is) and *its* — ***It's a big dog.*** ***Its legs are long.***

Subject pronouns						
I	you	he	she	it	we	they
Possessive adjectives						
my	your	his	her	its	our	their

this, that, these, those

We use ***this*** to talk about one person/thing near us, and ***that*** to talk about one person/thing far away.

This (here) is my bedroom. ***That (outside) is the garden.***

We use ***these*** to talk about more than one person/thing near us, and ***those*** to talk about more than one person/thing far away.

These (on my feet) are my shoes. ***Those (there) are your shoes.***

Unit 2

have got (affirmative and negative)

The Present Simple of ***have got*** has two forms: ***have got*** and ***has got***.

I/You/We/They have got lots of friends.
He/She/It has got long legs.

We use ***have got*** to talk about someone's things or to describe someone or something.

I've got a new bike.
You've got a hole in your shoe.
Brad has got red hair.

We use the short form in everyday language.

Long form						
I have	you have	he has	she has	it has	we have	they have
Short form						
I've	you've	he's	she's	it's	we've	they've

Be careful with ***it's*** *(it has)* **got** and ***its*** (possessive adjective).
Look at that dog! It's got a big mouth and its teeth are very sharp.

The negative is ***haven't*** *(have not)* ***got*** or ***hasn't*** *(has not)* ***got***.

Affirmative	
I've/You've/We've/They've got (I/You/We/They have got)	an American cousin.
He's/She's/It's got (He/She/It has got)	an Italian name.
Negative	
I/You/We/They haven't got (have not got) He/She/It hasn't got (has not got)	blue hair.

have got (questions and short answers)

We make questions by putting ***have/has*** before the subject, and then ***got***.

We don't use short forms (*I've*, *you've*, etc) with affirmative short answers.

Questions			
Have Has	I/you/we/they he/she/it	got	any food?
Short answers			
Yes, I/you/we/they have. Yes, he/she/it has.		No, I/you/we/they haven't. No, he/she/it hasn't.	

indefinite articles *a* and *an*

We use ***a*** with singular nouns that start with a **consonant** sound (*b, c, d, f, g, etc*).

a book ***a cat*** ***a dog*** ***a friend*** ***a girl*** *etc*

We use ***an*** with singular nouns that start with a **vowel** sound (*a, e, i, o, u*).

an apple ***an email*** ***an ice cream*** ***an orange*** ***an umbrella***

We don't use ***a*** or ***an*** with plural nouns (apples, books, cats, etc).

can

Can has the same form for all subjects *(I, you, he*, etc*)*. The main verb after ***can*** is in the **bare infinitive**.
I/We/She/etc can make/do/go/etc ...

We use ***can*** to talk or ask about ability.
She can sing very well. ***Can you speak Italian?***

We also use ***can*** to make and answer requests.
Can I use your pencil, please? – Yes, you can.
Can you help me, please? – Yes, of course I can help you.

The negative of ***can*** is ***can't*** *(cannot)* and it is the same for all subjects.

We make questions by putting ***can*** before the subject, and then the bare infinitive of the main verb.

Affirmative		
I/You/We/They/He/She/It	can swim.	
Negative		
I/You/We/They/He/She/It	can't (cannot) swim.	
Question		
Can	I/you/we/they/he/she/it	swim?
Short answers		
Yes, No,	I/you/we/they/he/she/it I/you/we/they/he/she/it	can. can't.

Unit 3

present simple (affirmative and negative)

We use **Present Simple** to talk about things that are always true, things we do often or that happen often, etc.
I watch TV every evening.
You know my friend Cara.
It snows in winter.
On Sundays we go to the beach.
My cousin lives in Spain.

In the affirmative, we add **-s** to the verb after *he*, *she* or *it*.
I/You/We/They like chocolate. ***He/She/It likes chocolate.***

With verbs that end in ***-ss***, ***-sh***, ***-ch***, ***-x*** and ***-o***, we add ***-es***.
misses washes watches fixes goes
With verbs that end in a **consonant +** ***-y***, we change the ***-y*** to ***-ies***.
study studies carry carries

In the negative, we use ***do not*** or ***does not*** and the bare infinitive of the main verb. We DON'T add ***–s*** or ***–es*** to the main verb.
The short form is ***don't*** or ***doesn't***.
I don't like history.
Ivan doesn't speak Spanish.

Affirmative			
I/You/We/They He/She/It	like/love/hate likes/loves/hates	rock music.	
Negative			
I/You/We/They He/She/It	don't (do not) doesn't (does not)	make	a lot of noise.

Grammar Explorer

like/love/hate + nouns & *-ing* words

After **(don't) like**, **love** and **hate**, we can use nouns *(chocolate, music, etc)* or *–ing* words.
I like films. I also like reading.
My brother doesn't like fashion and he hates shopping.
We love food but we don't like cooking.

definite article *the*

We use ***the*** to talk about a specific thing or group. It is specific because:
* there is only one *(the Earth, the Moon, the sky, etc)*
The sky is clear today.
* we explain, describe or understand clearly which one we mean
The boy next door is my friend. *(Which boy? The boy next door.)*
That's my mobile – the blue one. *(Which one? The blue one.)*
This is a good film. The actors are very funny. *(Which actors? The actors in this film.)*

object pronouns

We can use **object pronouns** after the main verb.
Can you help me, please?
Are you in this photograph? I can't see you.
Brad is my cousin. Do you know him?
That girl is in my class, but I don't like her.
I can't find my book. Can you see it?
Do you want to watch us dance?
Those are my sweets – don't eat them!

Subject pronouns						
I	you	he	she	it	we	they
Object pronouns						
me	you	him	her	it	us	them

Unit 4

present simple (questions and short answers)

We make questions by putting ***do*** or ***does*** before the subject, and then the bare infinitive of the main verb. We DON'T add ***–s*** or ***–es*** to the main verb.
Do you like football?
Does she go to your school?
Does it rain a lot here?

In short answers, we don't use the main verb.
Does she live in New York? – Yes, she does.
Do they study physics? – No, they don't.

Questions			
Do Does	I/you/we/they he/she/it	play computer games?	
Short answers			
Yes, I/you/we/they Yes, he/she/it	do. does.	No, I/you/we/they No, he/she/it	don't. doesn't.

questions with *Wh-* words

We use **question words** when we want more information than *yes* or *no*. We begin with the question word, followed by ***do*** or ***does***.

What	***What does she collect? – Fossils.***
When	***When do you play tennis? – Every Wednesday.***
What time	***What time does the match start? – At 4 o'clock.***
Where	***Where do your grandparents live? – In Mexico.***
Why	***Why do you collect fossils? – It's interesting.***
How	***How do you go to school? – By bus.***

adverbs of frequency

We use **adverbs of frequency** to talk about habits or how often something happens.

100% ←――――――→ 0%
always *usually* *often* *sometimes* *never*

> Adverbs of frequency go before the main verb.
> ***She often goes to parties.***
> ***They always have lunch at one o'clock.***
> **BUT** they go after the verb ***be***.
> ***It is usually warm in the summer.***
> ***We are never at school on Saturdays.***

Unit 5

countable and uncountable nouns

Countable nouns are nouns we can count – e.g. *one* ***laptop*** (singular), *two* ***laptops*** (plural). When the subject is plural, the verb is also plural.
This laptop is quite slow. ***Those laptops are really fast.***

Uncountable nouns are nouns we can't count (***water***, ***snow***, etc). They haven't got a plural form. When the subject is an uncountable noun, the verb is singular.
Water is important for the Earth. ***Snow comes from the sky.***

> We don't use *a* or *an* with uncountable nouns.

present continuous (affirmative and negative)

We use **Present Continuous** to talk about actions that are happening at the moment when we speak, or around this general time.
My friends are travelling to Sri Lanka today.
She is living in Barcelona at the moment.

We form the Present Continuous with **am**, **are** or **is** and the main verb with **-ing**.
I am reading a good book at the moment.
You/We/They are having lunch now.
He/She/It is sitting in the garden.

> With verbs that end in a **consonant + -e**, we change the **-e** to **-ing**.
> chas**e** chas**ing** danc**e** danc**ing**
> With most verbs that end in a **single vowel + a consonant**, we double the consonant and add **-ing**.
> w**in** win**ning** g**et** get**ting**
> With verbs that end in **-ie**, we change the **-ie** to **-ying**.
> l**ie** l**ying** d**ie** d**ying**

We form the negative by adding the word ***not*** after ***am/are/is***. The short forms are the same as for the verb **be**.
I'm not feeling very well.
You aren't listening!
My web cam isn't working properly.

Affirmative			
I'm You're/We're/They're He's/She's/It's	(I am) (You/We/They are) (He/She/It is)	studying	for a test now.
Negative			
I'm not (I am not) You/We/They aren't (are not) He/She/It isn't (is not)		studying	for a test now.

present continuous (questions and short answers)

We make questions in Present Continuous by putting ***Am/Are/Is*** before the subject, and then the main verb with **-ing**.
Am I doing this the right way?
Are you listening to music?
Is it raining outside?

In short answers we use ***am/'m not***, ***are/aren't*** or ***is/isn't***. We don't use the main verb.

Questions			
Am Are Is	I you/we/they he/she/it	reading?	
Short answers			
Yes,	I am. you/we/they are. he/she/it is.	No,	I'm not. you/we/they aren't. he/she/it isn't.

there is/are with a, some, any

We use ***there is*** (singular) and ***there are*** (plural) to describe what is in a place. In the affirmative, we use ***some*** with nouns in the plural.
There is a desk in my bedroom.
There are some posters on the walls.

The negative form is ***there isn't*** (singular) and ***there aren't*** (plural). In the negative, we use ***any*** with nouns in the plural.
There isn't a TV in my bedroom.
There aren't any flowers in the room.

We make questions with ***Is there*** (singular) and ***Are there*** (plural). In questions, we use ***any*** with nouns in the plural.
Is there a computer on your desk?
Are there any toys on your bookcase?

Affirmative			
There's There are	a some	book books	on the table.
Negative			
There isn't There aren't	a any	book books	on the table.
Questions			
Is there Are there	a any	book books	on the table?
Short answers			
Yes, there is. Yes, there are.		No, there isn't. No, there aren't.	

some and any with uncountable nouns

In **affirmative** sentences, we use ***some*** before uncountable nouns.
There is some food in the kitchen.

In **negative** sentences and **questions**, we use ***any*** before uncountable nouns.
There isn't any water in my glass.
Is there any ice in the fridge?

> We can use ***some*** in questions when we ask for something or offer something.
> ***Can I have some money, please?***
> ***Can I cook you some food?***

Unit 6

going to

We use ***be going to*** about future plans and predictions (what we think will happen).
I'm going to go to a concert in the park this weekend.
The sky is blue. It's going to be a nice day.

We form the **affirmative** with ***am/are/is*** + ***going to*** + the bare infinitive of the main verb.
I'm going to study hard before the exams.
We are going to start tennis lessons next week.
Karen is going to make a cake for the party.

> Be careful with ***be going*** (Present Continuous) and ***be going to go***.
> ***I'm going to Meera's house now.*** (Present Continuous)
> ***I'm going to go to Meera's house tomorrow.*** (*going to*)

Grammar Explorer

We form the **negative** with ***am/are/is*** + ***not*** + ***going to*** + the bare infinitive of the main verb.
I'm not going to do your homework for you!
Brad and Harry aren't going to play basketball this evening.
It isn't going to rain tomorrow, I'm sure.

Affirmative			
I'm You're/We're/They're He's/She's/It's	(I am) (You/We/They are) (He/She/It is)	going to	have a party.
Negative			
You/We/They aren't (are not)		going to	have a party.
He/She/It isn't (he is not)			

We make questions by putting ***am/are/is*** before the subject, and then ***going to*** + the bare infinitive of the main verb.
Am I going to win the race?
Are they going to visit their grandparents?
Is Meera going to come to the party?

In short answers we use ***am/'m not, are/aren't*** or ***is/isn't***. We don't use the main verb.
Are you going to meet your friends? – Yes, I am.
Is Brad going to go to Paris? – No, he isn't.

Questions					
Am Are Is	I you/we/they he/she/it	going to		make	breakfast?
Short answers					
Yes,	I you/we/they he/she/it	am. are. is.	No,	I'm not. you/we/they aren't. he/she/it isn't.	

possessive 's'

We use **possessive *'s'*** to show who or what something belongs to.
Where is the dog's food bowl? (It belongs to the dog.)

We use ***'s*** after a person's name, even if it ends in ***s***.
This is Anna's book. (It belongs to Anna.)
Do you like Charles's shoes? (They belong to Charles.)

We use ***'s*** after a singular noun.
That is my friend's house. (One of my friends lives there.)

When the noun is plural, the apostrophe (') goes after the ***s***.
That is my friends' house. (Two or more of my friends live there.)

BUT when the noun has an irregular plural, we use ***'s***.
This is the children's room. (It belongs to two or more children.)
Young people's hairstyles are strange. (the hairstyles of young people)

possessive pronouns

A **possessive pronoun** replaces a **possessive adjective + noun**. The possessive pronoun is the same for singular and plural nouns.
These are my shoes. (possessive adjective + noun)
They are mine. (possessive pronoun)
Do you like my hairstyle or hers? – I like yours.
Is this his shirt? – Yes, it's his.
Those aren't their bags – they're ours. Theirs are over there.

Possessive adjectives					
my	your	his	her	our	their
Possessive pronouns					
mine	yours	his	hers	ours	theirs

Unit 7

past simple *be*

The **Past Simple** of the verb ***be*** is ***was*** and ***were***.
I was often ill when I was a small child.
He/She was very nervous before the exam.
It was hot and sunny yesterday.
You/We/They were very tired after the lesson.

The negative is ***was not*** (***wasn't***) or ***were not*** (***weren't***).
I wasn't happy about the news.
He/She wasn't at school on Monday.
You/We/They weren't hungry at lunchtime.

We make questions by putting ***was*** or ***were*** before the subject.
Was I a fat baby?
Were you/we/they late for school this morning?
Was he/she excited about going on holiday?
Was it a good book?

Affirmative		
I You/We/They He/She/It	was were was	at home yesterday.
Negative		
I You/We/They He/She/It	wasn't (was not) weren't (were not) wasn't (was not)	at school yesterday.
Questions		
Was Were Was	I you/we/they he/she/it	asleep at midnight?

Short answers					
Yes,	I you/we/they he/she/it	was. were. was.	No,	I you/we/they he/she/it	wasn't. weren't. wasn't.

past simple regular verbs (affirmative)

We form the Past Simple of regular verbs by adding ***-ed*** to the verb. This is the same for all subjects.

I/He/She wanted a new computer, but it was very expensive.
We/They borrowed your mobile yesterday.

With verbs that end in ***-e***, we add ***-d***.
lik**e** like**d** us**e** use**d**
With verbs that end in a **vowel + *-y***, we add ***-ed***.
st**ay** stay**ed** pl**ay** play**ed**
With verbs that end in a **consonant + *-y***, we change the ***-y*** to ***-ied***.
t**ry** tr**ied** wor**ry** worr**ied**
With most verbs that end in a **single vowel + consonant**, we double the consonant and add ***-ed***.
f**it** fit**ted** trav**el** travel**led**

We use Past Simple to talk about:
• actions, events or situations which started and finished in the past.
We stayed in a really nice hotel in Vienna.
• habits in the past.
My parents travelled a lot when they were young.
• actions in the past which happened one after the other.
He washed his face, brushed his teeth and walked down the stairs.

There are some irregular verbs in English. We do NOT form the Past Simple of these verbs by adding ***-ed***.

Present:	**come**	**do**	**get**	**go**	**have**	**make**	**see**
Past:	**came**	**did**	**got**	**went**	**had**	**made**	**saw**

See Vocabulary Explorer: Page 111

Unit 8

past simple (questions and short answers)

We make questions in the Past Simple by putting ***Did*** before the subject, and then the bare infinitive of the main verb. This is the same for regular and irregular verbs, and the same for all subjects.

Did I/we/he invite Matty to the party?
Did you miss your dog while you were away?
Did he/she/they go to the new disco?

We can use **question words** to ask for information. We begin with the question word, followed by ***did***.

What did he buy? – A pair of jeans.
When did you go to Italy? – Two years ago.
What time did he arrive? – At 4 o'clock.
Where did I leave my mobile? – On the kitchen table.
Why did she go home early? – She wasn't feeling well.
How did you get to school this morning? – By bus.

In short answers, we use ***did*** or ***didn't***. We DON'T use the main verb.

Did Brad like England? – Yes, he did.
Did they cook dinner? – No, they didn't.

Questions			
Did	I/you/we/ they/he/ she/it	send	an email?

Short answers					
Yes,	I/you/we/ they/he/ she/it	did.	No,	I/you/we/ they/he/ she/it	didn't

adverbs of manner (regular and irregular)

Adjectives describe nouns, and adverbs describe verbs – that is, they say how someone does something. We form most adverbs by adding ***–ly*** to the adjective.

He is a careful driver. He drives carefully.
It's a quiet printer. It prints quietly.
It's a slow computer. It works slowly.

There are some irregular adverbs that don't end in ***-ly***:
well hard fast early late high low straight
They are good dancers. They dance well.
You're a hard worker. You work hard.
She's a fast runner. She runs fast.

past simple (negative)

The **negative** of the Past Simple is ***did not*** and the bare infinitive of the main verb. This is the same for regular and irregular verbs, and the same for all subjects. The short form is ***didn't***.

I/You didn't look at my photos.
He/She/It didn't hear the phone ringing.
We/They didn't think his invention was important.

Negative			
I/You/We/They He/She/It	didn't (did not)	know	the answer.

NATIONAL GEOGRAPHIC LEARNING | CENGAGE Learning

English Explorer Student's Book 1
Helen Stephenson

Publisher: Jason Mann
Project Manager: Alistair Baxter
Development Editor: Alistair Baxter
Assistant Editor: Manuela Barros
Product and Marketing Manager: Ruth McAleavey
Senior Content Project Editor: Natalie Griffith
Production Controller: Tom Relf
National Geographic Liaison: Leila Hishmeh
Art Director: Natasa Arsenidou
Cover/Text Designer: Natasa Arsenidou
Compositor: Ioanna Ioannidou
Audio: EFS Television Production Ltd

Acknowledgements

The publisher would like to thank Robert Crossley for writing the True Story and Project pages.

The Publisher would also like to thank the following for their invaluable contribution: Nick Sheard, Karen Spiller and Liz Driscoll.

ISBN: 978-0-495-90861-6

National Geographic Learning
Cheriton House
North Way
Andover
Hampshire
SP10 5BE
United Kingdom

Cengage Learning is a leading provider of customized learning solutions with office locations around the globe, including Singapore, the United Kingdom, Australia, Mexico, Brazil and Japan. Locate your local office at: **international.cengage.com/region**

Cengage Learning products are represented in Canada by Nelson Education, Ltd.

Visit National Geographic Learning online at **ngl.cengage.com**
Visit our corporate website at **www.cengage.com**

Photo credits

The publishers would like to thank the following sources for permission to reproduce their copyright protected photographs:

Cover photo: (Alaska Stock Images / National Geographic Image Collection)

pp 5 (Shutterstock.com), 7 (Rob Byron/Fotolia.com), 11 (Jason Edwards / National Geographic Image Collection), 12 (Shutterstock.com), 12 (Photos.com), 14 (Photos.com), 14 (ranplett/iStockphoto.com), 14 (Halina Yakushevichi/Stockphoto.com), 14 (digitalskillet/iStockphoto.com), 15 (Shutterstock.com), 16 (Shutterstock.com) 16 (Photos.com), 18 (John Prior Images/Alamy), 18 (Shutterstock.com), 18 (David Plummer/Alamy), 20 (Jean Blondin/Reuters), 21 (Sarah Leen/National Geographic Image Collection), 22 (Shutterstock.com), 24 (Cat London/iStockphoto.com), 24 (Renee Lee/iStockphoto.com), 24 (Jane Norton/iStockphoto.com), 24 (2009 Marvel), 24 (2008 Jupiterimages Corporation), 24 (Shutterstock.com), 26 (Shutterstock.com), 28 (Mark Raycroft/Minden Pictures/National Geographic Image Collection), 28 (Nina Kaiser/BigStockPhoto.com), 28 (Claudio Rossol/BigStockPhoto.com), 28 (Ramona Smiers/BigStockPhoto.com), 28 (Joel Sartore/National Geographic Image Collection), 29 (Joel Sartore/National Geographic Image Collection), 29 (Dan Helms/National Geographic Image Collection), 30 (Shutterstock.com), 32 (Shutterstock.com), 33 (Gordon Gahan / National Geographic Image Collection), 34 (Shutterstock.com), 35 (Shutterstock.com), 36 (MJ Kim/Staff/Getty Images), 36 (Connan/Bayerel/Corbis KIPA), 36(Jamie Painter Young/Corbis), 37 (Bill Hatcher/National Geographic Image Collection), 38 (Shutterstock.com), 38 (Photos.com), 39 (Shutterstock.com), 40 (Joe Gough/BigStockPhoto.com), 40 (Magdalena Bujak/BigStockPhoto.com), 40 (Liz Van Steenburgh/BigStockPhoto.com), 40 (Helen Sherwood-Taylor/BigStockPhoto.com), 40 (2008 Jupiterimages Corporation), 40 (objectif saveurs/Fotolia.com), 40 (Paul Chesley/National Geographic Image Collection), 40 (Rosmizan Abu Seman/BigStockPhoto.com), 42 (Shutterstock.com), 43 (Todd Gipstein/National Geographic Image Collection), 44 (John Todd/isiphotos.com/Corbis), 44 (Shutterstock.com), 44 (Photos.com) 44 (Matthew Ashton/AMA/Corbis), 46 (Richard Nowitz/National Geographic Image Collection), 46 (Ben Van Hook/National Geographic Image Collection), 47 (Shutterstock.com), 48 (Shutterstock.com), 49 (2009 Marvel), 50 (Shutterstock.com), 54 (Shutterstock.com), 55 (Jonathan Blair / National Geographic Image Collection), 56 (Tuy de Roy/Minden Pictures/National Geographic Image Collection), 56 (Shutterstock.com), 56 (Photos.com), 57 (Ralph Lee Hopkins/National Geographic Image Collection), 60 (Shutterstock.com), 62 (James L Stanfield/National Geographic Image Collection), 62 (Gordon Wiltsie/National Geographic Image Collection), 62 (Paul Chesley/National Geographic Image Collection), 62 (Michael S Yamashita/National Geographic Image Collection), 63 (Shutterstock.com), 64 (Shutterstock.com), 65 (Theo Westenberger / National Geographic Image Collection), 66 (Shutterstock.com), 67 (Shutterstock.com), 68 (2008 Jupiterimages Corporation), 68 (Jacom Stephens/iStockphoto.com), 68 (Eric Foltz/iStockphoto.com), 68 (Martin Allinger/BigStockPhoto.com), 69 (Shutterstock.com), 70 (Shutterstock.com), 71 (Shutterstock.com), 72 (Andrew Milligan/PA Archive/PA Photos), 72 (James P Blair/National Geographic Image Collection), 76 (Shutterstock.com), 77 (Maggie Steber/National Geographic Image Collection), 78 (Shutterstock.com), 78 (Photos.com), 78 (Michael Penty Photography/Rex Features), 78 (Travis Manley/Fotolia.com), 80 (PapaBear/BigStockPhoto.com), 80 (Richard Nowitz/National Geographic Image Collection), 81 (Clive Brunskill/Getty Images Sport), 81 (Anthony Harvey/Getty Images Entertainment), 81 (Sipa Press/Rex Features), 82 (Shutterstock.com), 82 (Photos.com), 84 (Allan Brown/iStockphoto.com), 84 (Jeff J Mitchell/Getty Images News), 84 (Jim Richardson/National Geographic Image Collection), 84 (Handout/Getty Images News), 85 (Shutterstock.com), 86 (Shutterstock.com), 86 (Becky Hale/National Geographic Image Collection), 87(Justin Guariglia/National Geographic Image Collection), 88 (Shutterstock.com), 88 (Photos.com), 90 (Shutterstock.com), 90 (Robert Clark/National Geographic Image Collection), 92 (Shutterstock.com), 92 (Photos.com), 94-95 (Shutterstock.com), 114 (Shutterstock.com), 115 (Shutterstock.com), 116 (Shutterstock.com), 117 (Shutterstock.com), 118 (Shutterstock.com), 119 (Shutterstock.com), 120 (Shutterstock.com), 121 (Shutterstock.com)

The following photograph was taken on commission © Heinle, Cengage Learning by MM Studios Ltd. pp 61

Illustrations by Dylan Gibson pp 4, 6, 7, 8, 15, 26, 89, 101, 102, 104, 108, 109, 113; Panagiotis Angeletakis pp 9, 10; Simon Tegg pp 18, 23, 32, 41, 72, 74, 95, 96, 100, 106, 112; Martin Sanders pp 19, 99, 106; Tim Kahane pp 25, 29, 38, 41, 45, 51, 52, 59, 74, 82, 94, 98, 103, 107, 112; Peter Cornwell pp 58; Eric Smith pp 67, 71, 91, 93, 98, 102, 105, 110, 111

Printed in Greece by Bakis SA
Print Number: 09 Print Year: 2018